Praise For White Knuckle Faith

White Knuckle Faith will challenge and inspire you. It is filled with true stories about a family that sets out to see God's faithfulness in the ordinary, practical things of life. They face challenges on every hand, and in the midst of those situations, they prove God great. This book will also apply directly to your own life, giving practical helps for how to live a walk of faith. I heartily recommend to you both Andy Huddleston and *White Knuckle Faith*.

Darlene Cunningham
Co-founder
Youth With A Mission International

Great reading and challenging! I'm reminded of Psalm 19:7b, "…the testimony of the Lord is sure, making wise the simple." God's ways work and they are applicable to each of our lives, regardless of our place or function. This is a powerful testimony of a family loving, discovering and practically applying God's ways. It speaks to this generation and will speak to generations to come. Read it and pass it on!

David Boyd
University of the Nations
Kona, HI

Andy Huddleston is the right man to address this issue. He has years of experience in dealing with the practical realities of ministry. He has become a "go to" guy when it comes to the hard work and faith of raising support and resources for ministry endeavors. He helps us see how God uses this practical aspect to help build our character and teach us how to trust Him more deeply. This is a must read for everyone venturing out into the wild and uncertain world of full time ministry.

Pastor Bill Lenz
Sr. Pastor, Christ The Rock Community Church
Appleton, WI

I have gained great respect for Andy and Susie as I have seen how effective and valuable they are in the work of the Kingdom of God.

Don Leetch
Co-founder, DaySpring Christian Card Company
Siloam Springs, AR

I've known Andy and Susie Huddleston for 32 years. From their early days in ministry to the present time, the Huddlestons have lived by faith, trusting the Lord for their daily livelihood. *White Knuckle Faith* has many wonderful testimonies of the Lord's faithfulness for those who are willing to take ventures of faith.

Andy's balanced approach — from his willingness to be a tent-maker, to encouraging the church to care for its own on the mission field — is timely exhortation for the Church today.

Dwight Douville
Senior Pastor, Calvary Chapel
Appleton, WI

For 25 years I have watched the lives of Andy and Susie Huddleston and their children. I have witnessed how God has taken them on a journey of faith and frust in Him. Through the years God has given Andy the ability to help and encourage others to depend on God for their provision and to help show in everyday life how they too can see God make a way where there seems to be no way. I encourage everyone to read and apply the truths in this book.

Frank Bullock
Director
Child Life International

Before I read the book, I watched the man. This book comes not from a theory, but from a life lived in the white knuckled territory. Andy is propelled by his love for God, his obedience to the Great Commission, and his love for both the missionary and the sender. I personally have been blessed and challenged by his life and teachings. It's time to sit down, relax and learn from a man who didn't just believe but set out to do what he read in God's word.

Randy Thomas
Director of YWAM All Nations
Trinidad, CO

White Knuckle Faith is not just another book on the subject of personal faith. This book is the true story of the Huddleston family who has chosen to live this way. The remarkable story in these pages captures the spiritual journey of a godly family's pursuit of the will of God. *White Knuckle Faith* will challenge you the reader, to examine your own measure of trust in God and to see this biblical truth in action: "without faith it is impossible to please God". Putting faith into action is the missing ingredient in many Christian lives today and I can tell you that you haven't really lived much of a spiritual life until you have experienced white knuckle faith.

Pastor Donnie Scarlett
Heritage Baptist Church
Huntsville, AL

An encouraging witness of trusting in God's word and seeing how God moves when you do.

Bruce Scott
Businessman
Oakton, VA

I strongly encourage everyone who has a heart for missions to read this book!

Andy Huddleston, whom I have known for over 15 years, has written an invaluable, time-tested and extremely practical manual on how to trust God on a daily basis. This book should be required reading for every pastor, youth leader and missions director.

Peter Iliyn
North American YWAM Regional Director
Salem, OR

"Many are called, but few are chosen." Andy is numbered among the called because he has chosen NEVER TO QUIT! His tenacious faith, his legacy of trusting God in trying circumstances and his courageous testimony will inspire your personal dream in God and strengthen your conviction to complete your assignment.

This book is not for quitters. This book is not for those who build a canoe when God asked them to build an ark. This book is for the few who dare to believe God for the impossible and who desire to learn how to live in the realm of His supernatural provision!

The inspiring stories in *White Knuckle Faith* will elevate you to action. The practical application will teach you how to trust God for the finances you need to succeed. Nothing is impossible for those who believe. This book will show you how.

Rev. Michael Morelli
International Evangelist
Founder, Morelli Ministries Int'l.
Tulsa, OK

White Knuckle Faith

Faith and Finances
Obeying God's Call
Stepping out in Faith
Going into all the World
Living by Biblical Principles

By Andy Huddleston

Mission Enablers Publishing
Kailua-Kona, HI 96740 USA

White Knuckle Faith
Published by Mission Enablers Publishing

Cover Design by Jane Ray, Fayetteville, AR
Book & Text Layout by Mark Spence, Kailua-Kona, HI

ISBN 0 9763449 0 4

Library of Congress Catalogue No. 2004117643

First Edition

For Information Contact:
        Andy Huddleston
        University of the Nations/YWAM
        75-5851 Kuakini Hwy # 194
        Kailua-Kona, HI 96740-2199
        andy@whiteknucklefaith.com

        www.whiteknucklefaith.com

Printed and bound in the United States of America

Dedication

This book is dedicated to my wonderful wife Susie and our seven incredible children.

Andy Huddleston grew up in a rural community in Tennessee. After some troublesome years as a teenager he gave his heart to Jesus, dropped out of engineering school and began a pursuit of God's will for his life. After leaving Bible college he and his wife joined Youth With A Mission. Andy has taught extensively across the US and parts of Central America, Europe and India. He is presently serving at the University of the Nations in Kona, HI. He also serves several international mission organizations. He and his wife live in Kona, HI, and have raised seven children.

Forward

Dear Lord... I really do want to serve you... but I have no idea where I will get the money... I know! If you really want me to go to Kenya, I trust that you will confirm it by giving me the Swahili language in the next half hour, and allow me to find a gold bar with my name engraved on it under my bed. That's it! That would be confirmation of Your will for me to be a missionary. Thank you dear Lord. Sincerely yours, Me.

Have you wanted to do something great for God, but were stumped because of the lack of finances, then tempted to pray one of those prayers of laying a fleece before the Lord, similar to the one above?

Andy Huddleston helps you wade through all the questions and emotions concerning faith and finances, but most importantly, he does this in a very practical, down-to-earth way. He doesn't just tell you *about* some grand ideas of "trusting God" — he shows you *how* to trust God.

And what is more important, he does this from his own life. He shares personally, from his own experiences.

Andy Huddleston has 28 years of experience as a

missionary, and he has seven children! They have never once missed a meal, and he has never failed to pay his bills. Andy has the authority from personal experience, and he has the faith to go with it. He has seen God come through time and time again.

Why not listen to a man who has "been there and done that!" *White Knuckle Faith* is going to guide you through the steps to being a man or woman of faith.

I think every Christian should read this book. In fact, I think after you read it, you are going to be so inspired to trust God, so full of faith for the impossible, that you are going to buy ten copies and pass them around to your friends and acquaintances!

God bless you.

Floyd McClung
Metro Christian Fellowship,
Kansas City, KS

Grateful Acknowledgments

I want to acknowledge with gratefulness the great men and women of God who have cared about my life. My grandparents George Robert and Viola Susie Huddleston lifted a standard of Christian character and the importance of God's word as the guide for life. My grandfather often looked me in the eye and said, "Son I've read The Book from lid to lid and let me tell you what it says." My mother and father, E. Winfred and Roy L. Huddleston, Sr., raised their six children with Christian values. Living before us the love of God and love for their neighbor, caring for the widows, reaching out to the poor and being commited to the church made a lasting impression on me. Dad and Mom were faithful church members. Dad was a deacon and layman who established churches to bring the gospel to families in poor or undesirable neighborhoods. Mom cared for us children and prayed for us regularly through our troublesome years. My wandering years gave way to a concerted effort by Mom, Dad and older brother Roy Jr., to "pray me into the kingdom". As soon as their prayers were answered, Roy, a minister, and his wife Kay took me into their home, and loved and discipled me intensely for two years. I often say, "Roy I don't know if I would be a minister and missionary today if it hadn't been for those early days of discipleship and a loving godly influence."

I still sign my letters to Roy, "fruit that remains".

While in Bible college I married Susan Grace McMahon and our burden to spread the gospel compelled us to join a missions organization — Youth With A Mission (YWAM).

Our mission adventure started in Elm Springs, Arkansas, at the Youth With A Mission training center under the leadership and direction of Rev. Oren and Inez Paris. They took us under their wing and discipled us for years. Their 17 years of love, friendship and discipleship built into us a solid Biblical foundation. We'll be eternally grateful for Oren and Inez.

Godly grandparents, parents, faithful men and women of God, loving friends, and particularly our *prayer and support team* have strengthened us to continue on in missionary service through the "thick and thin" of life's struggles in raising a family and being full-time in a faith ministry. Heaven will tell the story.

God bless you!

Special Thanks

My daughter Grace rewrote my entire manuscript and was the driving force behind seeing my first draft written, while Susie helped with critiquing, editing and more rewriting. Thanks to Jannie Rogers' training at her writing seminar. A special thanks to Svea Peterson Braum for the final rewrite of the manuscript.

Thanks to my sister Diane Gay Huddleston-Holt for her encouragement to get the testimony and teaching published.

Thanks to Mike and Katie Crow, Terry and Donna Keith, Oliver W. Bivins, Steve and Donna Collier, and many others for words of encouragement and counsel.

Thanks to Hans and Gunilla Bauman, Robert Evans, Ben Lenz, Michael Morelli, Mark Spence and Pam Shipp for reading the manuscript and giving valuable comments.

Thanks to Susie's parents Bob and Rita McMahon for enduring through some tough years with us.

Thanks to Tom and Cindy Patrick for being inspiring and believing in our testimony.

Thanks to my dear friends John and Jane Ray for their friendship, encouragement and years of serving together in YWAM.

A special thanks to Don and Leola Leetch and Bruce and Mary Scott for your invaluable pastoral care, wisdom, counsel, belief in us and encouragement through the years when things seemed impossible.

It all has been possible, and will continue to be possible because of our gracious heavenly Father, His son Jesus, and the indwelling Holy Spirit.

To God be the Glory!

Prologue

As a youth I would rise early in the morning. With my fishing rod and reel in hand, I would walk about a mile to Spring Creek. I was off to wade down the middle of that creek hoping to catch some hard-fighting small-mouth bass and perch. I could feel the warm murky creek water swirling around my legs as I pushed upstream. I had a cheap stringer hanging off my belt for the "nice ones" worth keeping. Sometimes I would step into a deep sinkhole on the creek bottom and get soaked up to my chin, but that was just part of the risk with this type of fishing. My biggest fear was failing to see the vicious water moccasins that lurked in the muddy water. I was always ready to leap back onto the bank before one of them lunged its fangs into my leg or, worse still, my backside. But that was half the fun, and the hope of delighting my mom, dad and brothers with my prize catch was well worth the risk. This was my formula for a great Saturday morning.

Heading off to obey God's call on my life was another risk worth taking. Stepping out into God's unknown path for me was like stepping into that creek water with its deep sinkholes. A desire to please Jesus has kept me moving forward by faith. Refusing to fear the unknown is that thrill of adventure that keeps me disciplined, getting up, grabbing my gear and walking that mile to do the next thing God directs.

I want to challenge you to embrace that personal journey that God has set before you. Throw yourself 100% into the vision with passion. You will not be disappointed as you discover He has gone before you and made a path for you to follow. God is the author and finisher of your faith. The adventure is waiting for those who will take the first step and trust Him.

See ya on the adventure!

Andy Huddleston, 2004

Table of Contents

Chapter 1

DISASTER AT SAN BERNARDINO

"…and lo, I am with you always, even to the
end of the age." Matthew 28:20b

The sickening, hollow crunch of twisting metal and shattering glass split the air as the misguided truck slammed into our travel trailer with destructive strength, forcing our van off Guatemala's jungle-lined highway.

Rain pelted our windshield in the brief silence that followed as my wife, brother and six children including our 12-year-old niece wakened to the reality of what had just happened. A quick look in the side mirror told all.

"Oh God, the travel trailer," I heard my own voice whisper. "It's gone." I turned quickly to check on the children. Jessica, our youngest, had fallen and bumped her head, but her cry was already winding down as Gracie, the eldest, comforted her.

"Somebody crashed into the travel trailer. Stay here," I said in a voice void of emotion, opening the door and stepping out into the rain. The scene before me was unbelievable. The travel trailer was demolished. The only part still hitched to the van was the travel trailer's floor on wheels with two propane tanks attached to the front end. Everything else was spread all over the ditch and highway. The top and sides were a twisted pile of rubble, the toilet hanging in mid-air by its copper plumbing tubes. All of our supplies, clothes, utensils, and toiletries were lying in soggy heaps everywhere amid the broken glass from the windows and mirror. A crowd of curious, dark-skinned spectators had already gathered. As I stood for a minute just taking in the reality of the mess before me, the peace of God descended upon me like a warm blanket, so real I could almost feel it physically. God was with us and I didn't have to be afraid.[1]

My eyes wandered to the opposite side of the road. There in the ditch lay a small crumpled pickup truck. I ran over to see if anyone there was hurt. The two cut and bruised Guatemalan men were conscious, although one was holding his arm and groaning. Once I was there I wasn't quite sure what to do. I couldn't understand a word anyone was saying, and even if I had known Spanish, it surely would have left me now. I seemed to understand that an ambulance had already been called, so I walked back across the road toward the van. The guys must have lost control as they sailed around the slick, wet curve. I was so thankful that none of us had been injured. If we had been a few feet further back, we could have all been killed.

Only moments before the crash, the kids had squealed with delight at their first tropical iguana sighting. I had been enjoying their inquisitive curiosity on our 60-hour road trip from Arkansas. We were three hours from our destination, Guatemala City, where we were to pick up a team of young college students joining a Youth With A Mission summer outreach. They were coming from the United States, eager to share the good news of God's love with war-torn Guatemala. But now, as I surveyed the damage, the seriousness of our situation hit me full force.

"Lord, what will I do? I don't know anyone here and have no way to get in touch with anyone. I don't speak any Spanish. Our food, clothes, bedding and everything we need is all over the road getting drenched. Oh God, send help."

I looked over to see a truck pulling off the highway and a thin, gray-haired, white man getting out into the downpour.

---

1. Matthew 28:20; Isaiah 41:10; John 14:27

He walked over to me and in a commanding tone said, "I've stopped to help. Don't say anything; just follow my instructions. Pick up everything that can be salvaged and load it into the back of my truck." As he went to back his truck into a more convenient position, I ran to the van to let everyone know what was going on. My brother Marc, niece Angela, and the older children jumped out to help while my wife Susie stayed in the van with the littlest ones.

I lifted my eyes from the pile of wet clothes I had been collecting out of the ditch to see police cars pulling up. The officers came up to me demanding my driver's license and the keys to my van. I knew what this meant. It seemed to be common knowledge among travelers in Latin America that after an accident, the officials confiscate the vehicles, and put the drivers in jail until the accident is settled. But Bill, the man who had stopped his truck to rescue us, interceded. Fluent in both English and Spanish, he asked them if it would be possible for us to finish getting all the things off the road and to his house before they confiscated the van and what was left of the travel trailer. They not only agreed to this but decided not to put me in jail if I would stay at Bill's home. We hurried to finish our task.

About an hour after the accident we were leaving the scene. As I followed the small truck loaded to the top with all of our junk, I couldn't help marveling at the way God sent someone to help us at the exact moment that we needed it. It was truly incredible. Bill told me his story later saying, "When I saw the accident, my first thought was, 'Hmph. Tourists.' There was no way I was going to involve myself. But as I proceeded to drive on by, I felt this strange, strong impression to stop. It was almost as if someone grabbed my steering wheel and made me pull over. I knew I had better help you."

He not only helped us get our stuff off of the road, but he also reassured us that everything would be fine. We would stay with him and his wife until the whole legal mess was cleared up and we could leave. That was quite a generous offer on his part, especially since he knew how sticky the Guatemalan legal red-tape was. One never knew how long it would take or how much money would be lost in the process. To make things even more complicated, the moment we crossed the border we had become uninsured. The U.S. company, because of all the wartime problems, wouldn't insure any vehicle going into Guatemala.

Bill, an American from Pennsylvania, was married to a lovely Guatemalan woman named Lupe (pronounced "Loo-pay"). She was truly gracious to us, welcoming all nine of us dripping foreigners into her nice home. After feeding us a good meal of beans and tortillas, she showed us where we could sleep, assuring us that we needn't worry about the huge mess facing us until the next day.

> But my plans were entirely different from my Creator's plans for me

That evening I surveyed the kids sprawling everywhere, their tousled hair covering sleeping eyes and breathing quietly. It is amazing how resilient children are, I thought. Would they remember these trips and the miracles we were watching God perform on a daily basis? Their lives were already so different from Susie's and my upbringing. Our wild adventure with God began only 12 years earlier. It didn't seem that long ago, and yet so much had changed. In my mind I could still see that lanky, longhaired, 17-year-old Andy, bent on living for himself. Having grown up in a Tennessee Baptist church, I had heard the message of salvation all of my life, but living it was the furthest thing from my mind and heart. Whatever it took to become a big-shot, that was my priority. But my plans were entirely different from my Creator's plans for me. Slowly His Spirit pursued my stubborn, selfish heart and showed me what was really in it. As I faced the ugliness of my sin, I realized how desperately I needed a Savior.[2]

With my repentance came a freedom and sense of destiny I had never before experienced. My desire to know God and to study the Bible expanded as I soaked in the teaching of my older brother Roy and in the sweet fellowship of the Christian friends I had been able to make. During this time I moved with Roy and his family to Wisconsin–a big change for this Southern boy! It was in this place I had previously only known as the "land of cheese and Old Milwaukee beer" that my world exploded in a whole new way of life.

One night after church I got a phone call from a friend who said he had been witnessing that weekend in a city about 300 miles away. To his amazement, he had bumped into someone who remembered me from a crusade some months ago. All she knew was my first name and that I was from Tennessee, but still she sat down on the sidewalk to write a short letter to me. Her name was Susie. As my friend read Susie's letter over the phone, I had no trouble remembering the dark-haired, blue-eyed girl with the simple, yet iron faith in Jesus. Christ had saved her, and she was going to serve Him. I also had no trouble convincing myself to keep in touch with her now that I knew where she was.

Our friendship grew and deepened into love. After a year of Bible college, waiting and seeking the Lord, we became engaged. So in the bright June of 1974, Susie and I were married.

Marriage was all we had hoped and dreamed (as well as a lot we had neither hoped nor dreamed, but accepted anyway). There was one problem though–one which at times seemed too impossible to face–we had no money. The recession during the 70's hit us hard, and as much as I tried,

---

2. Romans 10:9; John 3:16-21; I John 1:5-10

I couldn't find a steady job. No job, no savings, no home — just lots of hope in Jesus and faith in His promises. He would never leave nor forsake us. He cared more for us than for many sparrows.[3] If we'd seek first His kingdom and righteousness, all "these things" would be added unto us.[4] In other words, if we would love Jesus, seek to serve Him, and live by His example, He would take care of us, and all the "things", including finances, He would take care of. Even if we were faithless, He would remain faithful.[5] So with all our hearts we set ourselves to trust and obey. It seemed such a simple lesson, yet it was one we would carry with us all of our lives.

Somehow we managed to rent a small apartment, a second-story flat above Van's Shoe Repair shop. The smell of the glue used to repair the shoes, the sound of a hammer pounding, and an occasional groan from downstairs added a certain life and character to the old downtown building. Besides, after months of having no place to call our own, we were good and ready to call it "home sweet home." Who cares where you live, anyway, when you have hope and joy living inside of you?! Because the apartment had no mailbox, we made our own. We covered a cigar box with red and blue paper, wrote "U.S. Mail" on it and nailed it to the door jamb of our new home. We came to know it as "the blessed cigar box" because many times we would go to the box and find an envelope with the exact amount of money we needed at that exact time. Day by day, God was somehow meeting the needs we never announced.[6]

But an even tougher test of our growing faith was drawing closer every day. It wasn't just that the rent, the phone bill, the utility bill, and the car payment would all be due. So would our first baby! The big day arrived, and off we went to the very expensive hospital without even a dime to buy a cup of coffee while I waited for our little miracle to

---

3. Matthew 10:31 4. Matthew 6:16-34 5. II Timothy 2:13 6. Nehemiah 9:15; Isaiah 65:24

emerge.

That evening I became a father. My little girl, Grace, with her tiny heart-shaped lips, was healthy and beautiful. What can describe the joy as well as the sense of responsibility we felt as we together gazed, for the first time, at our daughter? We were now a family.

Leaving Susie that night, I went home with a full heart to our empty cupboards. I figured I had enough gas in my van to make it to the hospital and back a couple of times during the next few days. Susie and I had trusted Jesus and His Word every step of the way these last nine months. Our faith was simple. The Word of God was true. So why were we being tested like this?

I'm trusting You... but, Lord, if You don't come through, my name is 'Mudd'

"What will I do, Lord? My baby's here, the bills are due, we have hardly any food. I look for a job every day, but I just can't seem to find one. I'm trusting You... but, Lord, if You don't come through, my name is 'Mudd'."

The phone woke me up the next morning. The call was from the billing department at the hospital. They needed to see me right away.

The white-haired manager did not look too happy as he began his lecture.

"All right! We're going to handle this just the way any other business would. Do you buy your food at the grocery store without any money?"

I shook my head. Obviously this enraged man had no idea how seldom we'd been able to even go to the grocery store lately. His voice continued to rise, and his face grew redder as he continued his rampage.

"We aren't about to give you something you don't pay for either! And we're not going to let your wife and baby go home with you until you have $350 on my desk Monday morning. If you want your wife and baby, you just had better bring the cash."

I sat there completely floored. Trembling, I asked that the amount be reduced. Finally he agreed to $250, to be paid in 48 hours. Then I got out of there. I wasn't about to wait around for him to change his mind. I didn't know where I was getting my next tank of gas or meal, let alone $250. As I stepped into the elevator to take me up to Susie's room, I took a deep breath, looked up and said, "Lord, You heard the man!"[7]

As I stepped out of the elevator, I met the young daughter of a friend of ours who was on her way down.

"Hi, Andy! Your baby Grace is beautiful."

"Thanks, Bonnie."

She handed me an envelope and got in the elevator. Minutes later I was by my wife's side, marveling at our daughter's fingers and toes. As I told her what the "money-man" had said, I noticed her looking at my hand.

"What's in that envelope?"

"Oh, Bonnie handed it to me when we passed at the elevator."

"Open it."

There in the envelope was $150. Where would a 15-year-old girl get that much money? Could it be from her babysitting money? We didn't know, but one thing was certain: God had heard the man and was already beginning to answer our prayers, even some of the ones we hadn't had time to pray yet![8]

I got Susie and Gracie home by borrowing the rest of the needed cash, but even amid the joy of having my wife and daughter home, I felt the weight of having to pay that enormous hospital bill (multiple thousands of dollars). Despite the nagging fears, I knew the Lord would come through somehow.[9] Even though I didn't quite understand it, a sweet peace settled over us that first night together as a

7. Luke 12:24; Psalm 86:7; Psalm 91:15 8. Matthew 6:8 9. Psalm 20:6; Psalm 38:15

family in our little apartment.

The phone rang. It was Susie's Grandma Grace.

"Say, is now a good time for me to come over and see little Grace? I have a present for her." After checking with Susie, I assured Grandma Grace that she would be more than welcome.

When she arrived, Susie was resting in bed with baby Grace. Grandma seemed especially excited about the gift as she handed it to Susie.

"Open it, dear."

I was sure Susie wanted to just rip the package open, but she politely opened the card first. As she read the inside of the card, her eyes lit up and she took a deep breath.

"Oh, Grandma, thank you," she said sincerely. "Thank you so much." She quietly put the card back into the envelope, and opened the package. I wondered what the card said.

We visited as Grandma rocked her new great-granddaughter. And of course she was especially pleased that we had named her "Grace."

After we said our good-byes and Grandma was on her way home, I started toward the bedroom to ask Susie what the card said. She wouldn't wait for that.

"Andy!" she called to me. "Come here and look at this card!"

Actually, it was just a little note card that said, "The Lord Bless You Real Good!" But inside the envelope Grandma had put a check for $500.

"Praise God," I said still holding the check. "Your Grandma just made sure that the Lord blessed us real good!"

Early the next morning, the phone rang.

"Andy, are you ready to work?"

It was my former boss, ready to give me a job starting the next day. Work! And it was a good job too.[10] I could finally pour my time and energy into providing for my family. The haunting guilt of unpaid bills and unstocked cupboards was about to leave.

A few days later when I called home to check on everything, Susie greeted me with an odd story of receiving in the mail a $12 check from the bank. Maybe a promotional for getting a bank account for the new little Miss Huddleston? I'd check it out when I got home from work that night.

I stepped through the door that night feeling good about coming home after a day of hard labor. Susie seemed excited as I kissed her and baby Grace.

"I have to tell you something, Andy. After I hung up today I looked a little closer at the cashier's check and noticed the check wasn't for $12.00, but $1200.00."

My mouth dropped open.

"Are you sure? Let me see it."

She handed it to me, saying, "I called the bank to ask about the promotional and was told there was no such thing. When the secretary asked what the problem was, I told her we had received an anonymous cashier's check. She said the check is perfectly good and is ours to keep."

> The Haunting guilt of unpaid bills and unstocked cupboards was about to leave

We were full of awe that night as we thanked the Lord for His generous provision. We'd had no choice but to trust Him to meet our needs, and He'd overwhelmed us with more than we ever needed. He had taken care of that hospital bill faster than any insurance company ever could have. And we soon discovered that His blessing wasn't over. The "windows of heaven" remained open, and by the end of the week our small apartment was bursting with a washing machine and dryer, color television, bedroom suite, and a kitchen full of appliances and food–not to mention the total of $2,700 we

---

10. Colossians 3:23; I Thessalonians 4:11-12; II Thessalonians 3:6-15

had received from varied sources.[11] A sense of security swept over me as I reflected on all that had happened. God's Word was true and could be trusted. It seemed obvious that God was building and strengthening our faith. But why? What role would it play in our future?[12]

In the summer of 1976 we went to New Jersey to take part in a week-long rally called "The Spirit in '76." For months God had been opening our eyes to the needs around the world and to an occupation we knew little about — missions. A certain missions organization kept popping up. It was called "Youth With A Mission." Their motto was bold: "To Know God and To Make Him Known." Susie, huge with our second child, and I joined another couple in a trek to check out this YWAM group.

The week went by so fast. The theme had been, "Go into all the world and preach the Good News to all creation!" As each speaker, with conviction and sincerity, shared about God's command to each believer to GO, our own spirits, prepared by the work God had begun months ago, completely soaked it up. The fellowship with the believers we met there was sweet, and when the rally was over the flame the Lord had kindled was blazing even hotter in our souls.

One morning soon after, I awoke with a certain feeling of expectancy that God was about to break through with fresh direction for our lives. Jesus must have more for us to do than just pursue the American dream and go to church on the weekend! But lately it seemed the heavens had been closed when it came to getting direction from God. He knew our hearts and the longing to daily live our lives according to His will. We wanted to *be* Christians, not just *pretend* to be. My only question was this: Will I ever know that I know what God's *specific* will is for our family?[13]

Later that morning the mailman stepped off our porch to head down the street. Grace and Ben were wide-awake; the

---

11. Malachi 3:10 12. Ephesians 2:10; Hebrews 13:21,

activities of the day would soon be in high gear. So I gave Susie a little hug and bounded down the stairs to grab the mail. Breathing deeply of the crisp air as I stepped outside, I took a look around. The old house we now rented needed a lot of repairs, but we really did live in a nice neighborhood. Beautiful trees lined the streets, there were friendly neighbors...it did seem a good place to raise a family.

I reached in the mailbox and pulled out a letter. My pace back to the house quickened as I glanced down at the return address and noticed it was from Susie's sister, Katie, and her husband, Mike. They had been attending a missions college for over three years and, as part of their missionary training, were now in Ontario, Canada, serving as house parents in a home for Native American girls. Addressed to both of us, the letter promised to be full of news, exciting stories, and encouragement.

Susie opened the letter, and together we read it with all the pleasure we had anticipated. The Lord was moving in the lives of the various Native American girls, and Mike and Katie were growing also. Toward the end of the letter Mike began to share several scriptures dealing with the need to reach the millions of people all around the world who had never heard the gospel. Using verse after verse, he poured out his heart concerning his own continual realization of the need to freely share the truths with which he had been entrusted–the same truths that had set him free. Finally in closing he challenged us to search the Word of God and find out for ourselves God's command to His children.

---

13. Psalm 25:12-15; Psalm 38:15

One particular verse he had written out commanded my attention:

> "Go therefore and make disciples of all the nations, baptizing them in the name of the Father and the Son and the Holy Spirit, teaching them to observe all that I commanded you; and lo, I am with you always, even to the end of the age."
> Matthew 28:19-20

As I turned this last command of Jesus over and over in my mind, I realized that these words were just as much to Susie and me as they were to Mike and Katie. I continued to study my Bible and began to see how extensive God's plan of salvation is, and how clearly He called each believer to be a part of that plan. It seemed natural that anyone who had received God's grace would naturally want to share this gift with anybody who didn't have it.

"Susie, I won't make you go to YWAM, but it will take so much longer for you to become the person I created you to be if you don't go."

During the next few months, as Susie and I talked and prayed about our future, we became more and more convinced that it was God's will for us to go, to move out of our comfortable current life and do something radical for Him. The excitement from this realization became greater and greater.

As my anticipation grew, I began to notice a look of uncertainty in Susie's eyes. Where would we live? How could we make it financially? Would the children be safe? How would they be educated? And our families, we'd sure not see them very often. I could try all day to assure her with spiritual-sounding proclamations of faith. Yet I knew that for her to be at peace she would need God to speak directly to her own heart.

One evening as I sat poring over my collection of missions brochures trying to wade through the terms to figure out exactly what it all meant, Susie came in and sat down.

"The Lord spoke a verse to me," she said. That got my attention. She'd had her Bible on her lap, and now she opened it and said:

"While I was praying this morning, He showed me to help and support you in this new direction God is leading us and He seemed to be saying, 'Susie, I won't make you go to YWAM, but it will take so much longer for you to become the person I created you to be if you don't go.'"

Then she read to me from her Bible:

> "Truly I say to you, there is no one who has left house or wife or brothers or parents or children, for the sake of the kingdom of God, who shall not receive many times as much at this time and in the age to come, eternal life." Luke 18:29-30, Mark 10:29-31

Eyes shining, she went on to tell me that she didn't even mind leaving our little home in Wisconsin anymore. God would be our home, our security. But what was more, she felt the Lord had spoken to her heart that He did want to give our family–sometime in this present age–a house in which to raise our kids. In the meantime, she was content to trust Him and obey.

Release flooded my heart. Together in one mind and purpose, we could step out and pursue the calling we heard ringing so clearly in our hearts. We were going. Going where? Hmm. Didn't know yet. But we were going.

Chapter Two

ANGEL ON THE HIGHWAY

"Are they not all ministering spirits, sent out to render
service for the sake of those who will inherit salvation?"
Hebrews 1:14

I remember laughing as I met Susie's eyes over the
overturned hat she held out between us. What idiot chose
this life's destination out of a hat?

Our decision to go to Youth With A Mission closely
followed our determination to serve God full-time and obey
His command to "Go into all the world." We had heard a
lot about YWAM when we had participated in "The Spirit
in '76" rally some four months earlier. Several different
YWAM training base locations were represented there, so I
eagerly collected brochures from each of them to take home
with us. It was a fairly new organization, full of vision, life,
and opportunity to serve in almost any realm of experience.
What's more, it offered a "Discipleship Training School"
to teach new missionaries how to become the people God
desired for them to be. The school, known as "DTS,"
consisted of three months of classes followed by two months
on the mission field, learning by doing. With our decision to
GO already made, it didn't take us long to decide that YWAM
was the place. And I wanted to get moving soon. The only
question was this: Where should we do our training? I had a

lot of information about all the different YWAM bases, and no idea which one God wanted us to go to. Thus, the hat.

With a prayer in my heart I closed my eyes, reached in the hat full of brochures, and drew one out. I handed it to Susie. Looking down, she read: "Elm Springs, Arkansas."

"O.K.," I said with a grin, "I guess that's where we'll be going!"

Sound like a strange, ridiculous, terribly unspiritual way to make a decision? Maybe it was. But, shucks, the Bible says that every lot is cast, but its decision was from the Lord.[1] We guessed it was kind of like the story in Acts when the disciples cast lots to decide who would join the apostles in place of Judas. So we went for it! And our next job was to send our applications to this YWAM base of "our" choosing.

When our little family packed up and headed down to Tennessee to visit my folks over Christmas, we decided to swing by our handpicked future home, Elm Springs, Arkansas.

Sound like a strange, ridiculous, terribly unspiritual way to make a decision?

"Not to check it out to see if we really do want to obey the Lord," I explained to Susie as we plowed along in our old blue van, "but to see what the Lord is leading us into. You know, like Joshua's spies checking out Canaan before they crossed the Jordan."[2]

Finally, after driving most of the day, I spied the small green sign reading: "Elm Springs, Population 687."

"We're almost there, Honey," I sang out. Susie looked tired. We slowly wound our way around the narrow country highway whose scenery boasted an abundance of bare, wintry trees, dead brown fields, and an occasional cold and lonely-looking cow. It would be pretty in the spring. We passed (however briefly) through town, which mostly consisted

1. Acts 1:26 2. Joshua 2:1

of a gas station/convenience store; Ted's Barber Shop, a deserted and peeling white building with a false front (a relic of grocery-shopping days gone by); and a row of several houses (one front yard sporting a sign reading, "Hilly-Billy Trading Post"). We turned a corner, made our way up a long hill, and the paved road changed to a reddish-colored dirt road (well pot-holed). We soon saw a rather "rustic" sign saying "Youth With A Mission," turned right to enter the driveway, and there, for the first time, beheld our destiny.

There wasn't a whole lot to see. Directly in front of us was a large farmhouse that appeared to be under reconstruction. Beyond it were twin narrow buildings with tin roofs and chicken wire covering the windows. To our left was a huge animal barn, faintly red, with its roof sagging and visible stalls badly needing repair. Up the hill a ways sat a smaller, brown building also roofed with tin. Beyond all this were acres and acres of field. One glance told all: we were visiting an old, run-down chicken farm.

Our arrival was soon discovered, and we were ushered into a small room in the farmhouse. We were then given the grand tour by one of the few but friendly YWAMers on "base." The house, we were told, would be used for housing and office space. The two narrow buildings had once been one long chicken coop, but a tornado had ripped out the middle section several years earlier. Our guide led our small crew to the brownish building on the hill.

"And this is the 'brooder,'" he announced, "where the baby chicks were once hatched. When I first came, we had to shovel out a couple feet of manure, and now look!" He opened the door and I poked my head in. "We even have a cement floor! This place will be our meeting room and dining hall." We walked around the building, and he enthusiastically pointed down the hill.

"See that barn? That's where the families are going to stay."

His excitement was contagious. I could see it now: the farm house with the stairs to the second floor fixed and a new coat of paint... the chicken coops with some siding to cover the broken bricks and rough planks... the brooder – after putting the ceiling in, we could build cabinets and shelves in the kitchen... and the barn, dorms, apartments, and the loft as a classroom. This was the type of work I was really good at! Finally — my chance had come to pour my 50 hours a week into something I knew would count for God. In the meantime, before all the much-needed renovations took place, we could get by.

I reached over and squeezed Susie's free hand, the one not carrying a bundled-up baby, and turned to grin at her, expecting to see mirrored in her face the excitement I knew shone in my own. She looked as if she was about to cry. I glanced up to take in my surroundings once again, and, pulling my head out of the clouds, understood what she was thinking...

"We're going to eat in some sort of chicken house? We're going to live in a barn?"

"Why, Lord? What sort of place is this to raise little kids? We're going to eat in some sort of chicken house? We're going to live in a barn?" I gave her a quick squeeze, and almost as quickly entrusted her doubts to the Lord.

I couldn't wait to go back to Wisconsin and pack up all our stuff. Maybe I could ask to come a couple of months early to help get some of the buildings ready for classes.

"Susie," I said, scooping Ben out of her arms and planting a kiss on his fat cheek, "I think we're coming out of the Wilderness into the Promised Land!"

"Or maybe out of Egypt into the Wilderness?" she answered with a little smile.

We got back to our little home and immediately began

deciding what to sell or get rid of. We didn't really have a whole lot, so after selling our stove, refrigerator, dishwasher, washing machine and dryer to a friend, our second-story flat in the old house was pretty bare. A small trailer would easily haul all we owned.

We hadn't had much time. It had only been about a month since we visited Arkansas. But that was fine. We didn't need a lot of time to get things ready, and besides, if I'd had to wait any longer, I might have burst from excitement. The good-byes had been hard in some ways, but our family and friends could see our eagerness and were excited for us and happy to see us off. Now, all that was left was the last-minute packing and the loading of the U-haul trailer. I took a deep breath and whispered a word of thanks to the Lord.

The frigid air bit our cheeks as we hustled out to the van early the next morning. The forecast had predicted 28 degrees below zero. Brr! I could believe it. Susie had grown up in this kind of weather, and although I had learned to function in it, I didn't think it was such a bad deal for us to be led to a warmer place. Today in particular, moving south didn't seem bad at all.

I started the van and let it warm up a bit. Susie was tucking Grace and Ben in, and seat-belting them down for the long ride ahead of us. I hoped to get at least to St. Louis by nightfall, but with the trailer behind us, I knew I'd better take it slowly and carefully.

A sense of adventure filled my heart as I pulled out of the driveway. Here we were, off to meet a future uncharted, holding a destiny that even Susie's wild imagination couldn't dream up. We had refused to be limited by the "plain old facts of life," and now, as we stepped out in faith, we were only praying that He would use us and make our lives count for eternity.

We'd been on the road for about an hour. My eyes stayed glued to the highway. With the wind blowing like it was, I knew I needed to stay alert and keep a firm grip on the steering wheel. I stepped on the gas to take on a hill, but to my horror the acceleration quit altogether. I pressed the pedal again. Nothing happened. Frantically, I tried to figure out what was going on. The way the engine was choking out, it was almost as if there was no gas in the tank. But that couldn't be it. Earlier I had placed a piece of cardboard in front of the radiator to keep the air inside the van warmer. Maybe there wasn't enough air getting to the engine.

"The engine can't stop now," I groaned to myself as I pulled off the road. "We're in the middle of nowhere; with our two small kids in the van, and this negative 28 degree weather and 40-mile-an-hour wind, we're really going to be in trouble fast."

I turned to face Susie. She knew something was very wrong, but seemed wholly at peace about it all. She reached over, took my hand in both of hers and began to pray.

"Lord, we know You're with us and will take care of us. Maybe You could send down one of Your mechanical angels to fix whatever it is that's the matter with our engine?![3] Thanks for Your faithfulness to us, Father. Amen." The prayer may have been short, but it was sincere, and so we waited, expecting an answer soon.

I hopped out to see if taking the cardboard off of the radiator would help. When I got back in, the temperature inside the van had already dropped, and Susie was putting more clothes on herself and the children. Even with more air reaching the carburetor after I'd removed the cardboard, I still could get no acceleration. I sat back in my seat staring straight ahead. What would I do? Then an old red pick-up truck heading the opposite direction caught my eye. It slowed down and pulled over on the opposite side of the two-lane highway. A bearded man stuck his head out the

---

3. Hebrews 1:4

window and bellowed,

"What's the problem?"

"My van seems to choke when I accelerate and I can't make it up this hill," I yelled back.

"Here! You need this." He got out of his truck, jogged over to where our gas cap was, and dumped a can of HEET gas treatment in the tank.

"Let the engine run for about three minutes and then you'll be on your way." With that he tossed the empty can in the ditch, got back in his truck, and rode off.

Dumbfounded, I noticed I was still sitting in my van. Susie grinned and quipped,

"Maybe that's our angel."

"I guess we'll know in about three minutes," I returned.

I put my foot to the pedal and started to move off the shoulder and back onto the highway. Sure enough, the van started picking up speed, and up the hill and on our way we went, laughing and praising God.

"You know, Susie," I said thoughtfully, "I'd have said that the Lord sent His angel to deliver us if that man hadn't littered like that!"

"Well, maybe he didn't want us to know he was an angel, and will go back later and pick it up. You never know, Andy," she replied with a laugh.

Whoever it was, we knew God was with us and protecting us. He was the one leading us to Arkansas, and He would be the one to get us there—each of us in one thawed piece![4]

We kept driving through Illinois en route to St. Louis until, to our dismay, we saw a threatening sign: "ROAD CLOSED." My thoughts began to churn.

---

4. Psalm 121:7-8

"This road can't be closed; it's the only one going south!" I pulled into a nearby service station. The attendant told me that the road was closed for the next 80 miles due to the snow piling up on the highway.

"Why didn't I think of how flat this part of the state is?" I reprimanded myself with a frown. "I knew better than to come this way. What are we going to do? We only have enough money for gas and food, not unexpected motel bills." A man approached me, interrupting my thoughts.

"Where are you going?" he asked.

"St. Louis. Hopefully tonight," I answered, hoping I didn't sound as bleak as I felt.

"My family's been stranded for three days now. We've been sleeping in a high-school gym the last couple of days," he said. Great, just what I needed to hear. But, no, he wasn't finished yet. He had heard that there was a road open that went through a city called Peru. He wanted to try to get through, but needed someone to follow along behind in case of trouble. He finished with, "Why don't we try that open route, and then if either of us gets stuck, the other can go for help." That sounded like a good idea to me, especially with the load I was pulling. So Susie and I gave this new twist in our journey to the Lord, figuring that this must be His provision.[5]

Off we went with a complete stranger. As we followed along behind, every time he would come to a bad spot in the road, our new-found friend would tap his brakes to warn me to slow down and be careful. I rejoiced to see how well the Lord was taking care of us. Like a guiding light we were able to follow this man as we traveled through the night in that area we had never been before. Finally, after several hours, we began to move east toward the highway again. Only a few more miles, and we'd be back on the road heading directly south.

But soon we turned a corner, and there in front of us was

5. Proverbs 16:9

a gigantic pile of snow. There was no way around it. We sat, engines idling and exhausted minds trying to come up with a solution. We had by-passed the piled-up highway for hours, and now were stopped–just before finally hitting the main route again. I could've cried. Instead I just sat there staring at the snow bank as if to melt it with my weary gaze.

Then clearly, out ahead of us in the dark, there shone a light.[6] As it moved closer, I could see it was some sort of snow plow. I watched it as it slowly moved the mountain before us to the side of the road. The Lord was with us *every* mile of the long, tiring day, guiding us and guarding us.

We pulled into Elm Springs the next day. As we drove up the long dirt driveway of the base, I realized that we had just moved our family to YWAM with only two dollars to spare. We didn't really care, though. We knew beyond a doubt that our Father was faithful, and He not only knew our financial status but also the very number of hairs on each of our heads.[7] We were finally here, and we could clearly see that the adventures had already begun!

---

6. Isaiah 42:16 7. Matthew 10:30

Chapter Three

LORD, WHAT ABOUT THE MONEY?

"You do not have because you do not ask." James 4:2b

The sour reek of dirty diapers lingered in our second floor room up in the farmhouse. The rest of our dirty laundry would have made a significant pile on the floor of our tiny abode. It was high time we did some washing. Though we couldn't drive our van due to the lack of insurance and a current registration, I had been able to borrow a truck. So we had transportation to take us to the laundromat. The bad news was, we didn't even have a quarter to wash one load of clothes once we got there.

Stating the obvious, I announced, "Susie, we have to do our laundry," as if she didn't already know. "We need the Lord to provide five dollars right now. Come on; let's pray."[1]

We got down on our knees beside the bed and made this specific request to the Lord. Then we got up and finished getting our clothes together to take to the laundromat, expecting God to answer soon.

Moments later there was an urgent knock at the door. I went and answered it, and there stood our downstairs neighbor with a five-dollar bill in her hand and a wide-eyed expression on her face.

"God told me to give this to you right now," she said,

---

1. Matthew 21:22; Jeremiah 29:12

pushing the bill into my hand.

I shook my head in amazement and accepted the money with thanks. Susie had a triumphant smile that said, "I knew the Lord would come through!"

Our Discipleship Training School (DTS) began soon after that, and we quickly got into the flow of class, meals, and work-detail schedule. Susie found it hard to leave our babies so often with a sitter, but even with this and the various other inconveniences, we found our spirits growing in truth and a deeper faith being established in our hearts. Along with our 32 fellow students, we devoured the teaching and instruction with eagerness.[2]

One afternoon about halfway through our training, a worker from the office came and gave each of us our "balance due" invoice. Susie and I knew God wanted us in Elm Springs, so we had come despite our lack of money. After explaining our situation to the leadership, they agreed to accept us, to believe God for provision and to pray with us for the needed $2,400. We were trying to sell our van in order to pay the tuition, but with no progress in our efforts so far. It had been a couple of months, and we still had not been able reduce the huge bill. Now the printed reality was staring me in the face.

With my thoughts fully occupied, I was walking toward the door of the business office with the invoice in hand when a voice broke through behind me.

"Hey Andy! Do you do business with Tontitown Bank?" It was the lady from the office.

"No," I answered, a bit surprised at her inquiry.

She continued, "Well, somebody from the bank called us today, and asked that Andy Huddleston come by the front desk at the Tontitown Bank as soon as possible. They said you should bring your driver's license or some other kind of identification."

---

2. II Peter 1:2-11; II Timothy 2:22

I wondered what was going on. Why would the Tontitown Bank need me? Full of curiosity, I ran to tell Susie the news and then raced off to the bank.

I stepped up to the desk and identified myself to the bank teller. After checking my identification, she told me that someone, who wished to remain anonymous, had come in to the bank and left $1,000 for Mr. Andy Huddleston.

My mouth dropped open. Was this a dream, or what? We hadn't asked anyone for money and here God was using this mysterious someone to give us a huge gift.

The lady handed me a release form and a pen. Then, giving her head a slight shake, she opened a drawer and handed me an envelope containing $1,000 in cash.

My heart was full–God had provided nearly half of our tuition! I wanted to run and tell everyone I saw about God's mystery miracle. (I did, in fact, tell a salesman I met at a sports shop. He just shook his head in wonder.)[3] Since God was taking care of us, what was there to worry about?

> Since God was taking care of us, what was there to worry about?

Before we knew it, we were getting ready for our very first missions trip. We would be going to San Luis Potosi, a city of over a million people in central Mexico. We planned to distribute Spanish New Testaments to as many of its poor residents as possible. For preparation our leaders began to describe to us the country, its culture and its people. They told us of the difficult living conditions, the extreme heat and the precautions we must take to stay healthy:

"In order to avoid dehydration and possible heat stroke, DRINK LOTS OF WATER, but never any that has not first been purified. And never eat any food unless it's in a sealed

---

3. Psalm 89:15-16

package, or we give it to you. If you do, you run a high risk of getting amoebas and other parasites."

Wow! I could see the headlines now – "Huddleston dares the wild lands and fierce heat and takes on untamed Mexico for the kingdom of God!" I turned to Susie to catch her reaction to our orientation. From the look on her face, I could tell her thoughts went more along the lines of, "It's so hot that people dehydrate? You can get parasites just from eating and drinking water? What about our babies? They still put everything in their mouths. What if... well, what if they get sick and die? It has happened before... I don't know about this...."

Susie's fears were very real and valid.[4] We shared and prayed with our leaders and realized that we were committed to the journey of trusting God, whatever might come. He would protect our children, and He would protect us.

The day of departure arrived. I helped load our baggage complete with lightweight clothing and little hats to cover Grace and Ben's tender bald heads. Susie took the kids and situated them in the back of the old school bus nicknamed "the Boss", our golden chariot for the adventure. I thought that the way the old bus looked, one miracle would have already taken place if we simply made it down there! I climbed on the bus, took my seat with my family, and settled in for the long ride ahead.

On the second day of our journey we continued to make our way south toward the Mexican border. I noticed the scenery changing as the climate became hot and dry. The trees were shorter and more twisted, like large mangled bushes dotting the desert-like landscape. As we drew near the border, I noticed more and more Latin-Americans occupying this south end of Texas. Even though we were in the United States, billboards and road signs were written in both English and Spanish.

---

4. Isaiah 41:13; Proverbs 1:33

We went through customs and then past the last border checkpoint. We were now in Mexico. Since this was my first time to ever leave the United States, my interest and curiosity were high. Smiling, I glanced down at my two sweating children, thinking of how they wouldn't even be able to remember their first trip out of the country. I turned my attention back to the rattling window of the bus to get a good look at this country surrounding me.

If Texas had seemed a desert, Mexico surpassed it in drabness. The scrubby little trees and cacti sparsely interrupted the brown expanse with bits of green. The landscape certainly wasn't very impressive.

The moment we crossed the border I had noticed a marked change in the atmosphere between the U.S. and Mexico. It wasn't just the dark skin and Indian features of the Mexicans, nor the Spanish words covering the signs and walls. Driving deeper into the country, my eyes beheld the intense poverty of the Mexican people. Sitting under hastily assembled shelters, men and women would try to scrape together a meager living by selling fruit, meat, small trinkets or anything else they could find. When the bus would stop at an intersection, small boys would race into the street begging us to buy their "chiclets," Mexico's chewing gum. Old women sat in the sun weaving brightly colored blankets to sell at the market for little money. It seemed every house and business was fashioned of concrete and tin. The streets were covered with garbage, as if the people had ceased to see a reason to care anymore. It was hard to believe the vast difference a few miles could make between one country and the next. I felt shame at the worry I would sometimes feel at our own financial situation. Our lack didn't begin to compare to this all-too-real, life-threatening poverty that millions of Latinos faced every waking hour.

My heart hurt for the impoverished, oppressed people I saw around me. They seemed so worn, so utterly without hope. I felt Susie's hand take mine. Though it was hard to see their suffering, I was glad we had come. Maybe we could make a small difference, offer them a real hope.

The weeks of our time in Mexico slipped by, each day filled with new challenges to meet, trials to be overcome, and testimonies to tell of God's faithfulness. Upon arrival at San Luis Potosi, we and the 250 other YWAM missionaries there pitched our tents at the rural El Mosquite campground. With so many tents of various shapes and sizes sprawled out, not to mention the beat-up school buses, we looked like a gypsy band off the cover of National Geographic magazine.

But we were neither gypsy nor tourist. We were in Mexico with a simple goal: to give a New Testament to anyone who didn't have one (which seemed to be just about everybody). We started out on our Bible distribution project with excitement, knowing that the pages of these New Testaments carried the same good news of salvation that had transformed our own lives. We went in groups of two or three. It helped if at least one person in the group was able to read the Spanish "speech" that had been prepared to explain who we were and what we were doing. Very few of us spoke Spanish, so we relied heavily on these Spanish "cheat sheets" and used a lot of pantomime. If all else failed, we could always put the Bible in the person's hand and walk away. That, in fact, seemed to be my chief method of getting the Word out for at least the first few days. However, I soon discovered how friendly the Mexican people were and how they enjoyed our comical attempts at speaking their language.

We began in the city itself. The homes looked as if they were joined together by one continuous wall that stretched down the entire length of the street, sort of like townhouses, except the wall was drab and ugly and extended around the entire block. Here and there people had painted their section of the wall a bright pink, yellow, or turquoise to liven it up a bit, and some of the iron bars on the windows were scrolled in artistic designs. Not sure what to expect, we knocked at one of the old doors in the wall.

A cheery, round woman greeted us with a flow of Spanish. Of course we could do nothing but nod and smile and then proceed to haltingly read our cheat sheet. She listened patiently, occasionally correcting us to herself, and then beckoned us to come right in. She flung open the door to reveal a courtyard filled with flowers, sunshine, and trees with birds flitting in the branches. Her home was like a small apartment that had its own door to the courtyard. There were other apartments connected to the courtyard, and she gathered her neighbors from those apartments so that they too could receive a New Testament.

For weeks we walked mile after mile, freely giving God's Word and His love. Each door opened to reveal a new face, a different personality, another unique person with whom we could share the joy of God's love. Because Grace and Ben were still so little, Susie wasn't able to go out on Bible distribution as often as I did, but she really didn't seem to mind staying "home" with the babies. One of her big adventures was hand-washing all the laundry for our family of four–including diapers–in a big bucket with a rub-board. She was a trooper! We were really happy, with a supernatural joy and contentment because we knew we were doing exactly what God wanted us to do. This life of giving God's love to others, what so many term "missions," would be ours for the rest of our lives. God was aching to have a living relationship of love with each person He had created; yet people all over the world were still living lives bound in selfishness and every kind of oppression. How could we not be missionaries?

Early one morning I crept out of our tent to take a walk. I needed to talk to the Lord about a certain struggle in my heart. Here I was, a thousand miles away from home with only 50 pesos in my pocket, barely enough to buy two bottles of pop. It wouldn't be so bad if we hadn't spent all of our money, and now at the end of the trip we were running short. But we'd only had 100 pesos of spending money for the entire trip. I didn't even want to think about the hundreds of dollars we still owed for our tuition. I knew God could provide for our family. We'd seen Him do it. But right now it seemed that our needs were growing and our provisions were drying up.

I sat down near a local farmer's irrigation ditch and watched the trickle of precious water flowing by. It reminded me of the trickle of money we'd received since I'd left my job to become a missionary. I still had my wife and kids to support, and although she never complained, I knew Susie longed for the home she felt the Lord had promised her. Right now it seemed the fulfillment of that promise would be in the very distant future. Yes, we had "counted the cost" and were willing to do whatever was necessary to obey the call of God on our lives. But now we were discovering that "going into all the world" would cost real money — money to supply our basic needs, and then even more money to accomplish the work He had given us to do.

I began to pray, "Lord, I want to serve You, but I don't see how You're going to finance this missionary life You have destined for us to live. I want to be fruitful, but it is overwhelming to think of the amount of money it will take to do Your work. There are thousands of unreached peoples in far away places, millions to feed, tons of printed materials to produce, and millions of dollars needed just to train and send the few people who have been obedient to Your call. Where will all this money come from?"

Sensing His presence, I opened my Bible to the third

chapter of Titus. In the passage,[5] Paul told the believers there to help provide the needs of the men of God serving them. By doing this, they would be doing what was good and leading productive lives. God's people were to support God's workers. That made sense. And it fit right in with Romans 10:15; "How shall they preach unless they are sent?"

This explained why the traditional churches had organized programs to send out and support their missionaries. But frankly, I was more impressed by the great men of faith like William Carey, Hudson Taylor, George Mueller, and Samuel Morrison. These men were examples of obedient servants, their faith continually in action. Their awe-inspiring testimonies of supernatural provision convinced me that if the same God provided for them, He could provide for me too. The famous stories of the Bible seemed to center around this method of provision too ... Elijah and the ravens...[6] the multiplication of loaves and fishes...[7] the multitudes of Israelites crossing that terrible desert[8]—some say it took 30 railroad box-cars of food, and 300 tractor-trailer tankers of water to just provide the basics for that incredible journey!

> God's people were to support God's workers. That made sense.

So, did God want to provide for us supernaturally, or should we be supported by God's people? And then in Acts 18 it says that Paul worked as a tentmaker to finance his missionary work....[9]

The questions churned in my mind as I called out to God for understanding. I jotted down in the margin of my Bible the scripture references coming to mind so I could study them later, and then I got up, brushed the dirt off my jeans, and headed back to camp. I knew He was right there, listening to each question, and in His time, Jesus would bring

---

5. Titus 3:13-14 6. 1 Kings 17: 1-16 7. Mark 6:33-44 8. Exodus 13:17
9. Acts 18:3; 20:33-35

the answers.

Chapter Four

RELIEF FROM THE WRINGER WASHER

"...you will be enriched in everything for all liberality,
which through us is producing thanksgiving to God."
II Corinthians 9:11

I clomped up the rickety stairs of the old white house we were renting in Lebanon, Tennessee. Dust and sweat clung to my tired limbs — evidence of a long day at the construction site. Now what was I doing working construction in Tennessee? It was hard for me to head back to my hometown after having an incredible experience on the mission field in Mexico. I often asked myself the same question. I had the clear call of God and the desire to reach those without Jesus stirred continually in my being. But I also had debts to get free from, a growing family to care for, and the never-ending flow of bills to pay. So here I was, one year after tasting the life of full-time service to God, back hammering nails to make ends meet. "But what about the call, Lord?[1] What about the vision?" These questions left a dull ache in my heart that just wouldn't leave.

I walked in the house where Susie met me with a smile and a little story. "You know how I've been using that old wringer to do the laundry?" she began. I grinned at the thought of Susie bent over that ancient hunk of iron, coaxing it to wash the clothes. At the same time I felt kind of bad that

---

1. II Timothy 1:9; II Peter 1:10

she had to use it, that I couldn't provide something better for her. Between the kids, the house, and the laundry she had a full-time job. She really didn't seem to mind, though, and I loved her for it.

"Well, today when I was praying, the Lord seemed to be telling me to pray for a washing machine and dryer. That really caught me off guard. How could I pray for a washer and dryer, luxuries, really, after seeing the poverty of those people in Mexico? How could I pray for more when we already have so much?[2] Then God spoke to my spirit again — I'm sure it was Him: 'Susie, I want to give you a washer and dryer.' Tears began welling in my eyes. I was overtaken by God's generous, loving heart. Finally I asked Him to provide them, and do you know what He said?" Here she broke into laughter. "He said, 'What color do you want?!'"

"What color did you tell Him?" I asked.

"I was crying so hard; I just said, 'I don't care, Lord... white is fine.' Andy, God's going to give us a washing machine and dryer!"

I laughed with her in the wonder of it. She was pregnant again[3] and in the up-coming months could definitely use the help! Still, I couldn't help but wonder how God would do it.

After finishing DTS and leaving Arkansas due to lack of money I was able to sell our van and pay off the remaining tuition, as well as buy a used truck to help us get by. My dad had hooked me up with a contractor in Lebanon, Tennessee, and to work I went. But I was miserable. Susie and I dreamed of going back into full-time missions; maybe we could do our School of Evangelism (SOE) at YWAM in Europe or somewhere like that. Just the thought of doing what I knew we were destined to do breathed life into us. But with that breath also came reality. My job provided barely enough to live on; there would be no way we could save enough to go.

---

2. I John 3:21-22 3. Psalm 127: 3-5

Trips across the world just didn't fit in the budget. So on I worked, doing my best to be faithful to share Jesus with those around me, but honestly, I was discouraged.

Settling in, we hoped and prayed to be a part of a good church community. One day, as we were hunting the bargain racks for a new pair of shoes for our "big girl" Gracie, the salesman helping us began to tell us about Jesus and His salvation. We thought it was great to have a shoe salesman share his faith with us, so we asked him where he went to church. We figured a church where the individuals shared Jesus with those in their everyday life must really be on fire for the Lord! He gave us directions, and the next Sunday we went there.[4]

Trips across the world just didn't fit in the budget.

We pulled up in front of a nondescript double-wide mobile home with a few people chatting and laughing outside the door. Kids were running around seemingly oblivious to their "Sunday best clothes." Once inside, we were welcomed warmly by the people and as the pastor spoke and the service progressed, we knew this was God's place for us while we lived in Lebanon. Jesus was there and the Holy Spirit was active in these believers' lives, healing, speaking, and setting people free. Boy was it good to have fellowship again.

Several months passed. It was now July, and I was still working in construction, Susie was still using the old wringer to wash the laundry, and I was still frustrated waiting for God to let us go and be missionaries. The only pleasant thought was that any day now, I would personally deliver my third child in our own house, with the help of a nurse of course. Susie was overdue, and it would be our first home birth – a little scary, but, after researching into home births and praying, it seemed to be our best option. My mind chewed

4. Hebrews 10:24-25; Ephesians 5:17-19

on everything as I drove home from work.

When I got to the house, Susie met me with the news that we would be having company. Dean, a teammate from our DTS a year earlier, had called. A group from YWAM Arkansas would be coming through our area, and he wanted to know if we could set up a church for them to do some dramas. This was music to my ears! It would be great to see those guys again. I gave Susie a kiss, hoping our new little Huddleston would be born before they came.

Our hopes were fulfilled when only a few days later Corriene Elizabeth entered the world, her soft skin and blue eyes enchanting us all. The guys at work had been teasing me about having another baby; they said I should've bought a new bass boat instead. Ha! How could a "big-boy's toy" even begin to compare with the sweet, fresh life of my little Corrie?

Susie's grandma phoned with congratulations the next day. She wanted to know if it would be all right for her to buy Susie a new washing machine and dryer since there wouldn't be a hospital bill for her to help with. Grandma wanted Susie to pick it out herself. Remembering her conversation with the Lord, Susie asked,

"Can I choose whatever color I like?"

Grandma seemed a little puzzled by the question, but was sure that it could be arranged. There was one thing concerning her though: she wanted to be sure we wouldn't sell it or give it away, but would keep it and use it! Once again, the Lord had answered Susie's prayer.

The team from YWAM came and went, bringing with them life and joy that splashed all over Susie and me, like "fresh water to thirsty souls."[5] Seeing them revived our desire to put more of our time in direct service to God and led us to pray about returning to Elm Springs, Arkansas. We then called the base and found that an outreach would

---

5. Proverbs 25:25

be leaving for Mexico in January, and we were welcome to come and then do the classroom section of the SOE (School of Evangelism) following the outreach.

Of course, it was at this point that I received a "big-buck" job offer from the Hartsville Nuclear plant. This job would last for years and pay better than I had ever been paid before. But I wasn't even tempted to accept it. We knew, after praying, that going back to YWAM was God's will. I could never trade serving God, a thing of incredible value, for something so paltry as money![6] We had no more money than before, but who cared?!

A young guy, Phillip, from church decided he wanted to come with us to Mexico, so we all joined together for a big rummage sale to raise the funds for him to go. We didn't tell anyone that our own financial needs had not been met. We sold our truck to pay off some bills, but we had decided that we weren't going to tell anyone that we were broke. We felt led to follow in the footsteps of George Mueller and all those other great men of faith, who saw miraculous provision without telling a soul. So we stored our stuff and packed our suitcases, waiting for supernatural, miraculous provision. The fast-approaching date of departure was set: Monday, January 2, 1979.

That Sunday before we left, the church gathered around to pray for us and send us out.[7] I didn't mention a word about money and neither did anyone else. I felt that since we were not to share our need, the money was His problem, but still I couldn't stop the sinking feeling as I pulled out of the church driveway and headed towards my parents' house to have Sunday dinner with them. We had already packed up our house and I had been hoping that the Lord would use our church to help us at least a little. How would He ever provide? Could I take my family back to Arkansas without any money?

---

6. Matthew 6:19-24   7. Romans 10:14-15

That evening I called Oren, the director of the YWAM base in Arkansas, to ask him what to do. Could I come without the money? I had thought God would come through, but it looked as though He hadn't yet. I still was pretty sure He wanted us back in YWAM, but now I just didn't know what to do. Oren gave it to me straight: we really needed to have at least $800 to come. He encouraged me to call the pastor and be honest about our need. Since we had been going to that church for a year now and were being sent out by them, it would only be right for us to make them aware of the whole situation and give them the opportunity to help us.

I hung up the phone, conflicting thoughts and feelings crowding my mind and heart. I certainly didn't want to be a beggar, but what held me back from making our needs known? Was it pride? Or maybe I just didn't understand God's ways of provision? Was it even right to not let my church family know that we needed help? I wrestled with the questions, the doubts, the fears, and finally decided to call my pastor. Feeling a bit sheepish that

> He encouraged me to call the pastor and be honest about our need.

I had waited until the last minute like this, I took a deep breath and dialed his number.

"Hello?"

"Pastor? This is Andy. You know how we're supposed to be leaving tomorrow? Well...we don't have the money we need... I guess we're not going anywhere until we have about $800," I croaked into the phone. The compassion in his voice touched my heart as we talked for the next few minutes. He had never dreamed we didn't have the funds for our endeavor. Yes, he wanted to help, and if we'd come to church the following Sunday, he'd get moving on it.

That next Sunday the church prayed over us again and

sent us out again, this time with their financial blessing added to their spiritual blessing.[8] It was a humbling experience to see them give so generously to meet our need as soon as they were aware of it. I knew God had used a different way to provide this time; He was having other people partner with us, so that together we could share in the command of Jesus to go. We both, the receiver and the giver, were blessed to be able to work for (and with) the Lord.[9] I could only shake my head in wonder at all the Lord had yet to teach me as I walked in this path He'd set before us.

The next morning my family of five and Phillip packed into the old green car a friend had given us–another big answer to prayer–and we were off to Arkansas for the School of Evangelism, our second missionary training school. We knew we were in God's will and that He was pleased.[10]

We were so content: this truly was the life—absolute freedom from the driving force in our culture to have and to get stuff.

Our outreach to Mexico was great. We returned to San Luis Potosi, the city in central Mexico where we had been the year before, planning to do the same type of ministry as we had previously done. But alas, when we arrived, we discovered that the Bibles we were meant to distribute had not arrived. After waiting around for a couple of weeks to see if the New Testaments would ever show up, we prayed about what to do. We had heard that Operation Mobilization's literature distribution mission ship, Doulos, was at port in Vera Cruz, a coastal city about a day's drive away. Maybe we could help them with something.

Vera Cruz was a beautiful city right on the Gulf of Mexico. The warm weather, the ocean to swim in, and the

---

8. III John 5-8 9. I Corinthians 3:9 10. Ephesians 5:10

perfect view made it hard to remember that it was cold, wet and dreary back home. We sure didn't feel like we were missing much–poor, persecuted missionaries indeed! Our work consisted of making much needed repairs on board Doulos. It was such a blessing to be able to serve their ministry, and the Lord blessed us with joy as we did so.

Even the long bus ride back to Arkansas was great. The bus broke down and we got detoured by a washed-out bridge, but it all turned out to be a whole lot of fun! The food was good, the weather was gorgeous, none of our friends were driven nuts by our three lively youngsters, and it wasn't hard to have a good attitude! What can I say, we simply had a blast!

Upon our return to the base, we moved to a one-room "apartment" in the farmhouse, complete with our own bathroom! With Ben and Gracie's bunk bed and Corrie's crib, we really didn't have room for much else. Susie and I even slept on a piece of foam on the floor that we had to roll up every morning to make room. Regardless, we were so content; this truly was the life – absolute freedom from the driving force in our culture to have and to get stuff.

Our School of Evangelism classroom training was also superb. We were developing relationships with the people around us that would last for the rest of our lives and our understanding of God's ways was growing continually. Several principles which had emerged during our DTS were now being planted deep in our hearts during this SOE. I saw even more clearly; "clues" to knowing God's direction, His voice, and correction:

1. If a Scripture passage "came alive" during a time of Bible study, the Holy Spirit could be pointing it out for a reason.[11]
2. If one felt a heavy burden, a strong unexplained thought or feeling relieved only by prayer, it could be God making that impression.[12]

---

11. Hebrews 4:12; Psalm 119:105; II Timothy 3:16-17 12. Romans 8:26-27,

3. If one began noticing "divine coincidences," or lots of little circumstantial indicators coming together at about the same time, it might be direction from God.[13]

4. A strong dream, vision, or prophecy coupled with other scriptural understanding might be supernatural leading.[14]

5. In all these, it's important to remember that God never contradicts Scripture. He also uses those in leadership (parents, pastors, other leaders) to confirm His leading.[15]

It seemed that hearing God's voice, in most cases, was a process of discerning God's will. Knowing His desires for us frees us to DO His will, and of course this is the whole point of His showing it to us. As our hearts are open to God, the Holy Spirit is able to begin teaching us His ways and revealing His heart to us. It is all about our love relationship with our Heavenly Father rather than religious rules. As we walk with God He shines through our hearts, in our minds, and on our steps.

When the SOE ended, we were again faced with the question "What next?" God didn't really seem to be saying anything new, so we figured that we just had better keep doing the last thing we knew He had told us to do, which was to be a part of YWAM.[16]

Thus Susie and I became a part of the staff team at the Arkansas YWAM base. Such joy encompassed our young family as I began my new position as the base carpenter. Funny, wasn't it? Here I was doing nearly the same work as before, and getting no pay besides, and I was totally fulfilled. What can be said other than that it certainly did "surpass all understanding!"[17] There was no doubt: The very best place to be—for happiness, for safety, for provision, for life—is in the center of the will of God.[18] Nothing else could ever compare.

13. Ephesians 2:10; Hebrews 13:21; Acts 10:17-23 14. Acts 10:9-16; 16:9 15. Ephesians 6:1-3; Hebrews 13:17 (also see appendix for guidance article) 16. Proverbs 24:27 17. Philippians 4:6-7 18. Matthew 12:50

Chapter Five

MAKING A FEW BUCKS ISN'T SIN

"...nor did we eat anyone's bread without paying for it, but
with labor and hardship we kept working night and day so
that we might not be a burden to any of you..."
II Thessalonians 3:8

Grabbing a few of my tools and trying not to slam the
screen door, I stepped out of our yellow and white mobile
home. I walked the short distance to the wood shop where
I had been making furniture on Saturdays to sell in local
stores. Since I was still working full time as a volunteer
staff at YWAM, we really needed the extra cash that my
little furniture business brought in. The shop was located
in one of the chicken houses. Several hundred yards behind
the chicken houses was the "mobile home park", mainly
a few older mobile homes in an empty field. Sometime
earlier we had moved into the mobile home from our one-
room farmhouse "suite". We were so grateful for the extra
space: three small bedrooms, kitchen, living room and two
bathrooms. It was good timing too, because Susie was due to
have our fourth child in the upcoming months and we would
really need the extra space. Perhaps it wasn't the typical
American dream home–with its shaky construction, green
and orange carpets, sections of rotted flooring, and flapping
windowpanes–but then, we weren't pursuing the American
dream.

We had all we needed to be content and we had been really blessed in the past few years. It was a joy to be able to give the Lord 50 or 60 hours of my time each week and see Him never fail to provide for our needs through various ways.

One big need He had taken care of was our kids' schooling. Initially we had concerns about our children getting a good education if we stepped into missions. But, the year Gracie was to start kindergarten, I helped build our YWAM base's first school building. We bought an old chicken house, moved it to our property, and renovated it to establish Elm Springs Christian School. We built desks for the teachers and students, put in a large heating furnace, and hung the blackboards. The teachers and curriculum were chosen, and off went our little girl to learn about the great big world of reading, writing, and arithmetic.

As I sat in the sawdust-covered workshop reflecting on His goodness, I sensed the presence of the Lord. It seemed as if He wanted me to be still so He could speak to me. I had resisted the tugging of the Holy Spirit before and had always regretted later that I had been in too much of a hurry to stop and listen.[1] So this morning I decided to go back to the storage room and have some more time with God. I pulled up a five gallon paint bucket with a lid and, wrestling my little New Testament out of my pocket, sat down.

I spent several minutes flipping through my Bible, reading various "marked-up" favorite passages. Finally my eyes came to rest on one particular verse, Matthew 6:33: "Seek first His kingdom and His righteousness; and all these things shall be added unto you." I pondered this promise of Jesus for a few minutes. Since the beginning of our marriage the Lord had used this verse time and again to encourage and strengthen Susie and me to trust and follow Him with our all. And He had been good. He always made sure we had all we needed, and He had also given us great joy in serving Him.

---

1. II Thessalonians 5:19; Psalm 103:9

Then in the quiet of my heart I sensed the gentle voice of the Holy Spirit saying, "I'll show you a better way of provision if you'll let me. Go and tell my church all I have done for you. I will be with you, and my people will reach out to you." It was so clear. God wanted me to share my heart and efforts to minister with the church.[2] I knew that honest sweat to provide for my family wasn't wrong; on the contrary, it was the right and good thing to do. Making a few bucks wasn't sin. But I also knew now with certainty that, at least for a season, God had a different way for me. Right there, I decided that my furniture workshop, our only source of meager income, was closed.[3] It was as if the Lord was saying, "Close your doors, hang up your hammer."

The significance of what the Lord was directing me to do, and the enormity of the challenge, became clear. I had known that someone needed to stir up the church in regards to the great commission,[4] to make God's people aware of the needs of the lost, and to challenge them with the message of the kingdom. Now it was no longer a vague "someone" who was to do it, but me. I felt a fresh excitement. Most of the people in the churches I knew were like Susie and I were just a few short years ago. They envisioned missionaries as rough, wild-eyed fanatics jumping on a boat to Zimbabwe, destined to die a martyr from some dreaded disease. Of course, now I knew different, but there were still many in the church with such misconceptions of twentieth-century missions. It was time someone went to the Church to make them fully aware of the need for servants (not just evangelists, but mechanics, carpenters, computer experts–all skills) on the mission field,[5] for money, and for committed prayer warriors.

> It was as if the Lord was saying, "Close your doors, hang up your hammer."

---

2. I Corinthians 9:14 3. I Samuel.15:22 4. Ezekiel 40:4; Acts 20:27-28 5. Luke 10:2

Accompanying the thrill were questions and little fears concerning my own adequacy to do the job the way it needed to be done. I didn't have a Bible degree. I wasn't a real speaker. What would I say? Would they understand me? Would they accept me?[6] Still, in the midst of the questions and doubts of my own ability, I knew I had to obey. The story of Moses at the burning bush came to mind. When God told him that he was the one who would go and lead Israel out of Egypt, Moses argued against the plan on the basis of his own inadequacy. God, however, would have none of that and promised to be with him, to speak through him, and to anoint him to deliver the word and power of God to all of Israel and Egypt. It was God's project all along, and Moses' "inability" was no hindrance to God—as long as he obeyed.[7]

"Well, Lord," I prayed, stretching my legs as I arose from my cramped position on the paint bucket, "You're in charge of all this. I'm willing, and You're able."[8]

Later that day I stepped back to look at the finished product of my labor: a fine oak table, its wood softly gleaming through its new coat of lacquer. I'd deliver this piece, and after that they'd have to find someone else to refinish their antiques. My future Saturdays would be spent searching the Scripture, poring over missionary biographies, gathering information so I would be prepared to share with the church, and becoming "thoroughly equipped for every good work."[9]

One chilly January morning I poked my head into my bedroom to see if Susie was ready for her hard-earned breakfast. The sight that greeted me brought a proud smile to my tired eyes, and a sweet joy surged through my heart. There sprawled all over the crumpled covers of our bed was my family: Gracie, in her flannel nightgown and gleaming grin; Ben, his blond hair sticking out at all angles about his round face—for once without the mischievous twinkle in his eye—and Corrie, her chubby little hands and sweet

---

6. I Timothy 4:12 7. Exodus 4:10-13 8. Ephesians 3:1-19 9. II Timothy 3:17

disposition. They were all gathered around my worn-out but blissful looking Susie, who was nursing the newest addition to the Huddleston clan, Melissa Sue. I couldn't help joining them in marveling over her little red toes and tiny lips.

The past several months as I studied His Word, the Lord had been showing me how much He loved marriage and families–big families included.[10] He had designed the whole thing and desired for His families to be an example to the world of the love and care He had for all of mankind. I almost felt as if God were asking my permission to give me a large family. Already, with just four children, I was getting teased, questioned, and even rebuked for having so many kids. The one standard question that bugged me the most, probably because it was my own biggest question, was "But how can you afford them?" My usual "comeback" would go something like: "Well, if God could take care of over multitudes Israelites as they crossed the wilderness, surely my little family isn't that big of a problem to Him." Trusting God to lead us even in the size of our family was a challenge, but we were grateful to have the freedom of conscience to enjoy all of the children that God was giving us.

> "Behold, children are a gift of the Lord; the fruit of the womb is His reward. Like arrows in the hand of a warrior, so are the children of one's youth. How blessed is the man who has his quiver full of them." Psalm 127:3-5

Major changes in our routine happened that spring with the request from our base's director that I lead the upcoming DTS. This was the first time I had ever been placed in this type of leadership position, and from the start it was a challenging, stretching, and growing time for me. Our class was made up largely of families with children, with a few single adults sprinkled in for good measure. I discovered

---

10. Psalm 107:41-42

that to lead was really to serve, to lay down my own life for those I was leading.

After a productive lecture phase, we packed 17 kids and 20 adults into vans and headed to the border town of Reynosa, Mexico. Every day we'd go door to door in Reynosa giving away New Testaments, sharing through translators our testimonies in prisons, or presenting our puppet shows and clown skits in the local orphanage. Every night we'd return to our camp on the Texas side of the border to crash on our sleeping bags spread out on the floor, while trying to ignore the various small creatures that would crawl into bed with us.

After our two weeks at Reynosa, we made our way to Washington D.C., where we were put to work right away by David Wilkerson's inner city ministry. By day we were out on the streets passing out tracts and inviting people to the David Wilkerson crusade that would be held that night at a well-known abandoned gas station. By night we were working as counselors at the meetings.

The first day in D.C. I was teamed up with an African-American brother named James. As we took to the streets to invite everyone to the crusade that night, it didn't take me long to discover that I had a problem. My shoes didn't fit me well at all, my feet were killing me, and I had nearly two more weeks of tramping these streets!

"Hey, James, is there a K-Mart or something nearby?" I asked my big friend.

"What for?"

"I need to buy a pair of tennis shoes. These boots are really hurting my feet."

"Brother, you need shoes?" he asked and, seeing my affirmative nod, told me, "You don't need no cheap ones from K-Mart! Come on." He took me in his car to one of those huge skyscrapers only large cities can boast of. Leading me up several floors, he showed me into a gigantic shoe store.

His dark face beaming with a bright smile, he said, "I want to buy you the nicest shoes you can find. You know how the Bible tells it: 'How beautiful are the feet of him who brings good news!'"[11]

My heart swelled with gratitude to James and to our God. Through James I could see God's heart of generosity and compassion as I served Him obediently without complaining. I could sense God's pleasure in blessing me.

The next week and a half of helping with the crusades was incredible. The power of God moved as David Wilkerson spoke truth to the hearts of many in bondage. Scores of people went forward to receive Jesus and to be delivered from slavery to the devil, who had kept them bound for so long.

We served with the crusades in multiple states, sharing God's word and His love, until our last day of travel had finally come. Just a few more hours and we would be home. I glanced over at Susie, baby Melissa in her arms, staring wearily out the window. Everyone else in the quiet van was sleeping, reading or staring off into space. We would all be glad to be back on the old chicken farm. This had to have been the longest two months of my entire life.

A three hundred dollar steak dinner?

We arrived, bumping up the long dirt driveway to park in front of the brooder. After giving a few simple instructions to the team, I followed the herd down to the brooder to grab my mail out of our little cubbyhole mailbox before helping Susie and our little crew home to our beds. Walking back to where they all stood weary and waiting, I shuffled through the letters ripping open the interesting looking ones. To my amazement and excitement, one envelope contained a letter with a check for $300. Later, after the kids were tucked in and all was quiet, I read the letter.

"Dear Andy and Susie, This money is for the two of you

---

11. Isaiah 52:7

to go out and buy a steak dinner for yourselves." Laughing, I read it to Susie. A three-hundred dollar steak dinner? Probably not. But a short vacation as a family away from all other human beings? Now that would be nice! Together we thanked God for this unexpected blessing, seeing it as a reward from our Father for serving Him faithfully. He loves to bless His kids as they obey and serve Him out of love. I was reminded of Hebrews 6:10:

> "For God is not unjust so as to forget your work and the love which you have shown toward His name, in having ministered and in still ministering to the saints."

I breathed a prayer of thanks and steered my sleepy wife off to bed.

Chapter Six

"IS YOUR SEED STILL IN THE BARN?"

"Is the seed still in the barn? Even including the vine, the fig tree, the pomegranate and the olive tree, it has not borne fruit. Yet from this day on I will bless you."   Haggai 2:19

Listening to the muffled voices of prayers being lifted, I adjusted my position on the hard metal folding chair and glanced up. Instead of the regular Sunday evening service, our director, Oren Paris, had called for a time of intercession. We split into several smaller groups and began to pray. Letting my eyes roam for a moment, I could see the beauty and fervor of the Lord on the faces of these I was serving alongside.

Several minutes passed, and as the groups finished, a representative from each lined up in the front to share with the entire assembly what they believed the Lord was saying as they prayed. I put an arm around Susie and sat back to listen. One certain message seemed to be spoken again and again as each group shared: "You will make decisions for distant nations...". What could this mean? Why had God so clearly pointed this out to us? We couldn't help wondering. It wouldn't be long before we would begin to see the meaning of this new mandate.

A few weeks later, our base's "grapevine" buzzed with the news. Rios Montt, the President of Guatemala (1982), had called Oren, our director, with a plea: Would YWAM teams please come to Guatemala with as many people, Bibles, and other supplies as soon as possible? While I had been tramping all over the U.S. with my Discipleship Training School students, a friend of ours, Doug Mercer, had been blitzing Guatemala with his School of Evangelism students. President Montt, a Christian, had heard through his church of our missionary team. Recognizing the hope and stability the gospel of Jesus would bring to his war-torn people, he called to personally invite us to come and declare this good news. What more could we ask for? Oren, filled with zeal to storm through this door God had so providentially opened, was ready to mobilize our whole base, and even all of YWAM, to respond to Guatemala's plea.

I wanted to obey, to communicate, to speak forth His truth, but I wasn't really sure where to start.

I would soon begin leading the outreach phase of a School of Evangelism team, and I really started to get excited in my heart. In all probability our team would help in this massive effort to cover the nation of Guatemala with the gospel of Jesus. I did have one major concern, though. Susie was pregnant with our fifth child; the baby was due in the spring. I knew I couldn't truck her and all the kids down there at this time. It was still a few months away, and I knew the Lord would figure out something. He wanted what was best for Susie, my family, and my team, as well as for the country of Guatemala. So at the end of September I "kicked off" the School of Evangelism, blissfully ignorant of the hectic schedule ahead.

In the months after the Holy Spirit first encouraged me to help wake up the Body of Christ to the needs of His kingdom, the Lord had impressed one word continually on my mind: communicate, communicate, communicate.[1]

I wanted to obey, to communicate, to speak forth His truth, but I wasn't really sure where to start. I had already written hundreds of personal letters sharing with family, friends, and new acquaintances the vision the Lord had burned into my spirit. I spoke to those I'd meet, and if the chance came to speak in a church or some other gathering, I would rarely turn it down. I had even begun to send a newsletter every now and then. So I had been communicating, but still, it seemed the Lord was encouraging me to put forth a new effort.

God began showing me small areas in which I could improve. For example, I put a telephone in our mobile home, whereas before we had always used the public phone in the brooder. I also began to consistently send a newsletter out to everyone I knew. I became bolder in asking for opportunities to share in churches. I figured if God was telling me to speak, I must have a message. If I had a message, the church must need it. I concluded that it must be all right to humbly ask for an opportunity to preach. My whole way of thinking began to change as I realized that there are over 400,000 evangelical churches in the Western world. God really has got enough contacts and opportunities for all His missionaries.

As He raises up full-time workers for His kingdom, He's also preparing the hearts of His people to be challenged by these opportunities and He is preparing to support His people in prayer and resources. God's job is to open the doors and bring the "divine appointments." Our job is to GO AND DO IT –preach the kingdom, recruit laborers, touch people for healing, and not be ashamed to be "helped on the way"[2], financially or in other ways. My passion for communicating was increasing.

---

1. Ezekiel 40:4 2. Romans 15:24

Just as we were headed into a chilly November, I was called upon to join the Keith Green memorial tour for a few weeks. Leaving my School Of Evangelism with a substitute leader, I joined a small team of YWAM staff that followed Melody Green, the widow of the late singer and preacher, as she toured the country. Our responsibility was to assist in counseling and challenging young people to be radical for God, doing what they say they believe. With the memory of Keith Green's tragic death still fresh in our minds, we had an awesome opportunity. With the same zeal for the Most High God that Keith had, we tried to drive home the challenge for real Christians to "get out of their beds" and get moving for God.

Soldiers were everywhere brandishing their huge guns, ready to squelch even the slightest hint of rebellion.

Along the tour I connected with some Christians we had met at the World's Fair, and I received an invitation to speak to their church in South Carolina sometime in the future. That sounded good to me. I wasn't sure when it would work, but God would take care of the details like when and how.

I returned to Arkansas and enjoyed a peaceful Christmas only to be plunged into another hectic schedule in preparation for our SOE outreach to Guatemala. Susie and I had decided that I would go with the team and she would stay home with the children. If at all possible, I would fly back to visit about halfway through the outreach. After loading the students into two vans and packing a trailer, we were off. Tired from the strain of our frenzied outreach preparation, I gratefully settled down for the long ride ahead of us. Guatemala was many hours away.

Nine long days and zero showers later we crossed the Mexico/Guatemala border. It would be our last day of travel, for which all 30 of our tired, stinking bodies were grateful. I gazed out the window as we rode, taking in this country I had heard so much about. The brilliant green tropical surroundings were marred with the black evidence of guerrilla warfare. Soldiers were everywhere brandishing their huge guns, ready to squelch even the slightest hint of rebellion. The people's eyes reflected the fear and unsettledness of the atmosphere in which they lived day after day.

Right away we began our ministry: door-to-door Bible distribution, open-air meetings in the plaza each evening, and preaching in the churches on the weekends. Carol Gulledge, a fellow believer, joined us carrying a large wooden cross to attract attention and open doors for sharing the gospel message that the cross signified. The response of the Guatemalans was incredible to see. Using a translator or simply reading off a prepared Spanish "cheat sheet," we shared with the hurting people about God's love and His salvation. Often they would be moved to tears. When we'd ask them if they wanted to pray, they would fall on their knees or on their faces, crying out to God for help. I had never in my life witnessed such openness, even eagerness, for the gospel. I could see why God had so burdened our hearts for Guatemala at this crucial time.

The first month went by very quickly, but as time progressed, I really felt the need to return home to make sure my family was all right. I had been able to talk to Susie on the phone once a week since I'd been in Guatemala, but I knew that she needed me to come home, at least for a week or two, to help endure the long two months we would be apart. I really missed her, too. So, feeling a bit uneasy, I borrowed the money to buy a round-trip plane ticket to go home for two weeks and then return to finish the outreach with my team.

I looked out the small plane window as we touched down in Tulsa, Oklahoma, knowing that in just a few minutes I would be with my wife again, who would be at the airport waiting for my arrival. My thoughts turned wearily to my empty wallet, as I lifted a quiet groan to the Lord. "God, please don't let this be an extremely tight time while I'm home. Let us have fun, Lord...oh, and I've got to pay my friend back for this plane ticket too. Please, Father...", I pleaded.

Driving home that night, simply enjoying being with Susie at last, our financial situation again presented itself.

"Susie, we didn't get any extra money this month, did we?" I hopefully asked. She shook her head.

"No. Just enough to take care of the basics."

"Oh," I responded. I realized we would just have to trust God and not let our lack spoil the time we did have together. We drove on, cherishing our sweet time alone.

Late that night we pulled onto the base's driveway. On impulse, I braked to a stop in front of the brooder.

"Honey, I'm going to run in quick and check the mail, OK?" I said as I jumped out of the car. She gave me one of those "can't we please just go home" looks, but I shut the door and raced down to the dark, quiet building anyway. I grabbed the mail and headed back. Upon opening one of the few envelopes, my mouth dropped open in shock. I was looking at a check for $1000. I counted the zeros to make sure. Whoa! The Lord had poured this blessing into our laps, "pressed down, shaken together, and running over."[3]

My time home went fast, and soon it was time to fly back for the remaining few weeks of ministry. I felt bad about leaving my wife and kids again. Susie had been really sick almost the entire time I'd been home and, although this trial definitely made things more difficult, God's peace and joy had covered our home, and we had a blessed time anyway. I had even been able to write and send a newsletter while the

---

3. Luke 6:38

news was still hot! When the morning came for me to leave, though, Susie was still pretty sick. But what could I do? My plane ticket was bought already. In that moment, I was so grateful for a woman of faith like my wife, who trusted Jesus with me and was willing to let me be obedient even when it meant leaving her sick in bed with four kids, and pregnant with our fifth. I prayed fervently for her, kissed her tenderly, and reluctantly left to rejoin the team in Guatemala.

A few days later, when Susie called me at the pre-arranged place and time, I was heartened to hear a more encouraged tone in her voice.

"Andy, you know how I was so sick and in bed when you left? Well, after crying and praying, I went back to sleep. When I woke up again, I got up and was fine! God must have healed me!" Relief flooded my heart. God was taking care of my family, even when I couldn't be there.[4]

The rest of the outreach went smoothly. We assisted in unloading tons of supplies from one of YWAM's mercy ships, the Anastasis, to help ease the situation of so many Guatemalans suffering from the war. In addition, we had distributed over 20,000 copies of the Spanish New Testament, impacting the entire nation in ways that only God will ever know. The outreach ended and the SOE came to a close. What a full year it had been! Reflecting on all I had done during the last year, I couldn't resist sitting down and calculating how many miles I had traveled. I laughed at the final figure: I had gone over 35,000 miles in less than a year!

That spring we welcomed into our family our new daughter Jessica Joy. Even the lovely flowers bursting forth that early May morning couldn't compare with the beauty of seeing for the first time the face of my baby daughter.

---

4. Proverbs 3:5-6; Psalm 107:41-42

Seven shining faces would now fill the next family photo. I held tiny Jessica close to my heart and felt like a very wealthy man indeed.

*　*　*　*

My throat tensed as I tried to swallow, and my mind juggled with opening lines and imagined responses as I dialed the number penned in my little notebook.

"Hello, is Steve there?" I asked. It was about 9:00 in the morning and I was at a pay phone in southern Texas. In a few hours I would be crossing the border into Mexico, on my way to Creel to set up an outreach for about 30 high-school-age kids. But even this forthcoming adventure was far from my mind as I waited for Steve to answer the phone. Switching the phone to the other ear, I wiped the sweat off my forehead, simply the product of an already hot summer morning—or was it my nervousness?

I had met Steve Collier while on the Keith Green memorial tour the fall before. He hadn't been able to believe I had been working in missions full time with a big family and no regular salary for six years now. After further "checking us out," he and his wife, Donna, decided they would like to begin supporting us.

"Don't send us any of those newsletters," he said, "just give me a call if you ever need money. I make it, and I like giving it away."

Not long after that phone call, I decided to pack up the whole family to go visit them in Kentucky. We had a lot in common—a love for Jesus, kids, and a simple life style. We enjoyed our time together, and as we were pulling out to leave, he leaned in the window of our car putting $40 in my shirt pocket. "You know, this car really is too small for you guys," he said, "If you ever find a nice van you could buy, give me a call."

Well, I found the van and was now making the call. I sure hoped he really had meant what he said. I heard someone pick up the phone and growl a "greeting."

"Steve? This is Andy Huddleston."

"Andy. What do you think you're doing calling me in the morning like this? I'm in bed." My stomach tightened, and my mouth refused to utter anything intelligible. What would I say now? But wait. I could hear him laughing!

"Ha, ha! Almost got you there, didn't I? What do you need, Andy?" My heart slowly, thankfully, returned to its God-intended place. I gave a lame little laugh.

"Yeh, you sure got me. Actually, I'm calling about the van. You said you might want to help us buy one and, well, I found one. I checked it out and it seems to be in pretty good shape... it's $1600."

He said he'd pray about it with Donna, his wife. I could call him again when I got back from Mexico. Then he hung up.

A few weeks later I returned from Creel only to be welcomed by our empty trailer. Susie had taken all five of the children and had driven up to Wisconsin with her brother. I was to fly up to meet her in a few days to visit her family and a bunch of our friends in that area. In fact we had even planned a big dinner with all of them so we could share with them what we were doing and the vision we had. Still, with all this in the works, one of my main thoughts was, "I wonder what Steve decided about the van." So I called him again as he had requested. Hmm... it seemed he had forgotten about it, but would call me in a couple of days and let me know. I sat down feeling kind of dumb, but at the same time, willing to wait and see.

The phone rang. I glanced up at the clock on top of the refrigerator. It had been about 30 minutes since I had called Steve. I wondered who it could be.

"Hello?"

"Hi, Andy. This is Steve again. Donna and I prayed about it, and we want to buy your family that van. The check is in the mail." I wanted to jump up and down and whoop and holler, but of course I didn't. I thanked him as well as I could and saved my yelling for later. Wow! A van! God had given us a van! Our prayers had finally been answered, and we now had a vehicle adequate for pulling a little travel-trailer He had given us over a year ago. I couldn't wait to tell Susie.

I stood in the living room of Susie's parents' house, talking with her dad while I waited for her to get ready to go. Tonight was the night of the dinner we had been planning for months. About a year ago the Lord had given me the idea of having a sort of "missionary dinner" in which I could share with my friends in Wisconsin all that the Lord was doing with us and also ask them to consider supporting us financially. I talked to a couple of buddies from the area about it, and they said they thought it was a great idea, offering to help buy the food and find a place to have it. A few months before the actual date of the dinner, Susie and I wrote up 70 personal invitations asking for responses as to whether they would be able to attend. Then I had some return envelopes and "commitment cards" printed to pass out at the dinner. My mother-in-law, whose phone number we had written on the invitation, was shocked when nearly 50 people called and said they were coming. And now the hour had come.

Susie and I hurried out the door, leaving the children with grandma and grandpa. It wouldn't do to be late to our own party that we had thrown for ourselves!

Later that evening, when the meal was over, I stood up to speak. Excitedly I looked out into the sea of the faces of my friends from years ago. I began to share all we had been up to for the past six or seven years, and all the Lord had done in and through our lives. I reported on the trip I had just taken to Guatemala and was able to show a video of YWAM's vision to reach that nation with the good news about Jesus. And now the dreaded moment had come to ask my friends if they would pray about giving to us on a regular basis so we could continue serving God full time.[5]

This was the first time I had ever got up and point-blank asked a group of people to give to my ministry. My mind fumbled with what to say. What would they think of me? How would they respond? What right did I have to ask for money anyway? But wait a minute—did I just decide on my own to be a full-time missionary? Of course not! I had been willing to work a "normal" job, but knew the Lord had directed me otherwise. And in Luke 10:7 Jesus did say directly in regard to His disciples' full-time ministry that the laborer is worthy of his wages. Still...how could I be sure that "laborer" meant me?

> This was the first time I had ever got up and point-blank asked a group of people to give to my ministry.

I had spent a lot of time the last few years studying God's Word concerning the issue of missionary support, and as a result of studying and living according to what I found, I was beginning to see some of the answers. First, I knew that by spending all my time "in the ministry," I was right in the center of God's will.[6] Second, I knew I had a command from God to go to God's church and challenge them to be active in obedience to the Great Commission by praying,[7] going[8] and giving.[9] Third, I could see in Scripture how God had commanded the church to be generous, especially to those who had given their lives to minister the gospel.[10] I could see example after example of "God's missionaries" throughout the Bible who were supported in this way: the Levite priests of Israel,[11] Elijah the prophet,[12] Jesus Christ, the very Son of God,[13] Paul the apostle,[14] and Titus, a disciple.[15]

---

5. Titus 3:14 6.Matthew 7:21; John 6:27 7. Mark 11:17 8. Matthew 28:19-20, 9. II Corinthians 9:1-15; 11:7-9 10. III John 5-8; Philippians 4:10-19 11. Nehemiah 13:10 12. II Kings 17:8-17 13. Luke 8:3 14. Romans 16:24 15. Titus 3:12-14

Giving and receiving is all a part of believers loving one another .[16] Often, for the giver to discover the opportunity to bless another, the need must be presented plainly by asking. One thing was certain, though. It seemed a whole lot easier for me to be on the giving side rather than the asking side.

Looking squarely into their expectant faces, I stood that night to ask, letting my friends know that I needed their help. It wasn't easy. My voice broke, and I knew I couldn't go on without emotion. Before I completely lost it, a brother stood up and stepped beside me. Throwing an arm around my shoulders he addressed the group.

"Andy shouldn't have to get up and ask like this. We know what he's doing is good, and God is using his family. Come on. Let's give the way we know we can and should."

That night we received a generous offering, as well as commitments for a total of $300 in monthly support. As I obeyed God in going to the mission field, building relationships, serving the church, and humbly making our needs known, He was teaching me His ways of provision and meeting our needs.

The beginning of "Happily Ever-After"

Discipleship Training School – 1977

Riding the "Boss" to Mexico

Tampico – Mexican river ferry

The "automatic" washboard

The mobile home days

Building great friendships on Outreach

The house planning team

Andy, the "Builder"

Unless the Lord build the house...

God is faithful

Sharing the Word

Before the wreck

After the wreck

'Builder of All Things' Inspires Two-Story, Seven-Child Home

Heidi Stambuck

NEWS Staff Writer

The Andrew Huddleston family at Elm Springs is much bigger than Mom, Dad and seven kids. It includes people from around the country who pitched in four years ago and helped the Huddlestons build a house.

Huddleston, who is a counselor at International Missions Network Center (formerly Youth With a Mission) at Elm Springs, and his family are listed in today's issue of *USA Weekend*, the weekly magazine included in the Sunday edition of *The Morning News*. The magazine publishes an annual Family Spirit issue around Thanksgiving and this year's theme is "Families Working Together."

When he saw information about the issue asking for submissions, Huddleston, who wants to write a book on his missionary experiences, took it on as a writing assignment. In his letter, he described the family as unusual "in an ordinary sort of way."

He said when the family decided to take on the project of building a house, it wasn't a "pull yourself up by the boot straps" type of thing. It was more of a miracle brought about by a spirit of community as family.

The six-bedroom, two-story, two-and-a-half bath house with 4,000 square feet including the garage was built in four months and three weeks and is paid for because the labor and most of the materials were donated by people the Huddlestons have met and worked with over the years.

Huddleston said a particular Bible verse served as a theme for the experience and as encouragement. It was Hebrews 3:4, "For every house is built by someone, but the builder of all things is God."

Before moving to the spacious house, the family lived for eight years in a mobile home with two bedrooms. Two of the children slept on couches in the living room.

The family will soon mark their 15th year in Northwest Arkansas and, while they aren't missionaries in the traditional sense of working always in the field, it was only a few years ago that they realized they would be able to put down roots here. Huddleston's work with

■ See FAMILY/ Page 2A

The "Builder of All Things" article
(see Appendix I)

"She's worth more than 10,000 roses"

Chapter Seven

GOD, I NEED SOME BUSINESSMEN

"…'it is more blessed to give than to receive.'" Acts 20:35b

I stopped pacing the sidewalk in front of the pay phone outside the large shopping complex. Even so, shopping was the furthest thing from my mind.

"Of course I've got to call him!" I mumbled to myself as I deliberately walked over to the phone and reached for the receiver. I paused for a moment and then proceeded to dial.

I had met Bruce and Mary just a few months before while co-leading a high-school outreach with 34 teenagers to Creel, Mexico. Bruce and Mary had come with their teen-age daughter and son, and during the trip we struck up a friendship. Towards the end of the outreach we had one particular conversation that stuck with me. Bruce, a businessman, began to share with me what it was like to be called to give.

"You know, Andy, my biggest challenge is not the actual giving–I'm under Christ's lordship too, and as a successful businessman I am presented with the responsibility to give because God has made me able.[1] The difficult thing is to know where to give and to whom. Since I am a steward, my responsibility is not to just get rid of the money, but to invest it in qualified people and ministries actively serving God and helping to advance His kingdom." I listened as he

---

1. Luke 16:1-13

continued.

"But there's another thing. We businessmen are very busy and need practical communication; we can't always hear of the need while we're in our prayer closet. Andy, don't be afraid to ask...."[2]

As I pondered Bruce's words later, I began to realize that giving truly is a spiritual gift that the Lord gives to some in a special way. Often, along with this gift of giving, He will entrust what I call the "gift of making." When God burdens someone's heart to give, He will provide the substance with which they are able to fulfill this call to give.[3]

The receptionist answered my call. She said she'd put me through to Bruce's secretary. My mouth started to get dry, and I shifted my weight nervously to my other leg. What if he didn't consider me "qualified," or if he felt I was taking advantage of our brief friendship, or...whatever? I guess I'd never know unless I asked, would I?

My mouth started to get dry, and I shifted my weight nervously to my other leg.

His secretary sweetly greeted me and, after I told her my name, exclaimed,

"Oh! Bruce told me that any time you call I'm to make sure he gets the message right away." I couldn't believe my ears.

Just a few minutes later after a short friendly chat, I found myself taking a deep breath and bracing myself to ask the dreaded question.

"Bruce, because of our conversation while you were here, I felt it would be OK to share with you some of our needs, and to ask you to help us financially on a regular basis." To my relief he didn't seem caught off guard at all. "Actually I have been praying about it already, but I would like more time," he replied.

"Would it be all right," I asked, "if I called you back in a couple of weeks to see what you have decided?"

---

2. Luke 11:5-13; Romans 15:24; James 4:1-3 3. Romans 12:8; II Corinthians 8:14-15

"Sure, that would be fine."

When I called him back a few weeks later, he again received my call graciously.

"Mary and I prayed and have decided that instead of a monthly donation, we'd like to help build your support base by helping you put out a bi-monthly newsletter. If you'll just send us a rough draft including a main story, praise report, and financial report, as well as several pictures, we'll take care of the rest. We're excited about investing our money in helping you communicate to your friends, family, and donors."

I was stunned by their generosity. This was more than I had ever expected or even thought of! Not only would they be assisting us financially, but they would also be pouring their time and effort into seeing us fulfill God's destiny for our lives. God was providing the help I needed to communicate the vision of the kingdom of God effectively.

*   *   *

"How could they possibly have to 'go' again?" I groaned to myself, glancing back to see my five children ranging from eight months to eight years old, watching eagerly as I pulled our blue van off the main highway. While waiting for them all to finish their "business", I wandered to the back of the van to make sure our little travel trailer was still hitched securely. Today we should be arriving in Cheraw, South Carolina — that is, if we didn't have 80 zillion more "potty stops"! We had decided as a family to travel around and visit several different churches. Before we were through we would not only have gone to South Carolina, but to North Carolina, Tennessee, and New York, as well as to Washington D.C. to visit Bruce and Mary. I could tell already that it was going to be a long haul. I was glad we had the travel trailer so people wouldn't feel obligated to find housing for our large family.

What a blessing this travel trailer had been, especially since we now had a van with a rebuilt engine.

On a stop in South Carolina we shared with Maranatha Fellowship what God was doing in the world and how they could be a part. As we left the church they prayed for us, sending us out with their blessing, deciding to give us monthly financial support.[4]

As we visited churches of various denominations, I could see clearly the importance of continuing to build and renew relationships with them, especially the ones supporting us. God is interested in building the unity of His people. Prayer support, recruiting laborers[5] and financial provisions are all part of advancing the kingdom of God. The missionary has an important part in bonding churches together. The relationships must always come first. God's methods of providing for His laborers will often grow out of those relationships.[6]

We returned to Arkansas grateful that the Lord had gone before us. He had blessed our time there with other believers and had provided for our needs through their generosity.

*   *   *

The new year dawned, and with it something began to stir in me. The doors of Guatemala were wide open. God had made a way for our base's ministry there to expand to a permanent work. As I pondered what the Lord was doing there, a question began to form. Did the Lord want us go to be a part of the YWAM base in Guatemala?

Sometimes I wondered if we could even justify calling ourselves missionaries, when we lived in the United States on a renovated chicken farm in Arkansas. Who ever heard of a missionary like that? But then again, what was missions and what qualified a person to be a missionary anyway? What it really boils down to is not where I am, but where

4. III John 5 5. Luke 10:2 6. I Corinthians 9:11

my heart is. Am I committed to be an active part of God's plan to restore real people to Himself? Am I willing to do whatever God says to get all this accomplished? It's a life commitment to be obedient to God's leading no matter how glorious or un-glorious the job is. Could I consider myself a real missionary? Absolutely. I had a missionary call and a missionary heart, and I was being obedient to God's direction for my current part in His great commission. With those three prerequisites, I could be a missionary in Africa, Arkansas, or even the Antarctica!

Thirty-five college-age volunteers were fired up and ready to go to Guatemala to help establish the new YWAM work there. I was called upon to meet them on location in Guatemala City. As I looked forward to going that summer, I began to pray about taking the entire family with me. Susie, and especially my growing children, needed to have the same vision for Central America that I had. They needed to see, touch, and taste for themselves what God was doing. There we could take the time to listen to the Lord and decide about the possibility of moving to Guatemala permanently. Anyhow, the last thing I wanted was to be away from them for two months. In some ways I couldn't believe I was even considering such a wild feat. It would cost us hundreds and hundreds of dollars. We would be traveling through the heart of Mexico for days with no translator. It was crazy! But the more I prayed about it, the more right it seemed.

They needed to see, touch, and taste for themselves what God was doing.

All was quiet now, with Susie and me relaxing at our small kitchen table after tucking our five children into bed–quite an operation. I lifted my gaze to Susie who, after a hectic day seemed about ready to "hit the sack" for the night. I took a deep breath and presented the plan I'd been pondering.

"Susie, what would you think about all of us traveling to Guatemala this summer?" I really didn't know what to expect. Susie had expressed interest in Guatemala and had a desire to be involved, but to pack a nursing mom with four other children and an energetic husband into one vehicle to travel for a week would be no piece of cake. To my surprise she answered without hesitation.

"I've been expecting the Lord to send us on a trip like that. I think it would be great if we could take the kids on a mission trip." I looked at her as if I couldn't believe the words that were coming out of her mouth. She actually thought it was a good idea!

"Do you think this trip is the leading of the Lord, then?" I asked her just to make sure.

> "How else would I get the desire to stuff five active children into a van and drive all the way to Guatemala?!"

"It has to be!" she laughed. "How else would I get the desire to stuff five active children into a van and drive all the way to Guatemala?!" She had a point. I too had this completely crazy desire to go for it, knowing full well what it would entail. I would be driving 6,000 miles on narrow, bumpy Mexican highways. It would be my responsibility to find purified water that wouldn't make us sick and safe places to sleep at night. We had very limited Spanish skills: "How are you?" "Where is the bathroom?" and "Do you have a Bible in your house?" just about covered it. All of this didn't even include the vast amount of "dinero" (Spanish for "money") it would cost to get us there, sustain us for two months, and get us back safely. It truly was crazy–just the kind of "crazy" God was into.

A few nights later I sat down to write an "appeal letter" to all our friends, churches, and supporters. I expressed how, in light of our family's call to mission work, it seemed so important for all of us to go to Guatemala together. God had flung the doors wide open for our YWAM base to establish a long-term work there. I wanted Susie and the kids to be involved in this outreach. But currently we could not make this trip without the financial help of our friends. Would they give towards the $1,400 needed to cover the minimum budget for this outreach? Susie and I worked over the letter to make sure it truly conveyed our meaning and, with a prayer, we sent it out, once again trusting God to provide.[7]

However, our waiting was not passive. We had a lot of work to do! I began to get the van and travel trailer completely ready for the trip, equipping the vehicles with a sturdy set of radial tires that could make it across the rough Mexican roads. The travel trailer would need only a little work to house our family for the summer. Everything seemed to be coming together quite smoothly.

A few weeks before we were to leave, Susie and I received a phone call. To our surprise it was my brother Roy and his wife Kay, asking if we would like to take their twelve-year-old daughter, Angela, along with us. They thought Susie might need help with the kids while we were away, and Angela was a first-rate babysitter. She also had an interest in missions. Of course, we were glad to take her along with us, encouraged that she wanted to help. Since my youngest brother, Marc, also wanted to go, our van-load would increased to nine. Marc could help me drive and would be a good guy to have along, especially if anything went wrong. Everything seemed to be pulling together with one exception. We still needed money.

The appeal letter had been out for a couple of weeks now, with no major responses yet. As we continued making preparations, I felt a little like Noah as he built the ark.

---

7. Philippians 4:10-20

It must have seemed ridiculous to Noah to build a huge boat without an obvious body of water, but only the word of the Lord. In the same way it seemed silly for us to get ready for such a big trip with no money – just the word of the Lord. With only 20 days left, I knew God would have to either start sending in the money or show me that we were really offtrack.

Then little by little the "dinero" started to roll in. As the day of departure drew near, we still couldn't see how it would all come together, but we knew from past experience that we trusted in a faithful God.

Three days until the big leaving day. We had two extra tires for the travel trailer and one extra for the van. The sleeping bags were being gathered. The clothes and many household necessities were being moved to the drawers and cupboards in the travel trailer. We took a paper-diaper count: 384 packed and ready to "be filled". It would be a blessing for Susie to not have to wash all those diapers the way she had on previous outreaches! The kids had collected an abundance of books, crayons, travel games, and other little projects in anticipation of the exciting seven-day ride ahead. It looked as if we were ready to go. Only one slight problem: we were still $340 short with two days left, and I honestly couldn't see any place to cut the budget.

It was Wednesday morning, the day before we were to leave. We were still lacking $340, but as we prayed, Susie and I still felt that God would come through.

"I suppose we could go ahead and leave, and trust the Lord to finish providing even as we're on the road," I said to myself as I gathered everyone to go to the brooder for the prayer and worship service we always had on Wednesday morning. I especially wanted all of us to be there because this morning our director, Oren, and the rest of the base were going to pray for us and "send us forth."

We entered the brooder and could sense the sweet

presence of the Lord in the worship. We found a place for all of us to sit, trying hard not to jostle those less tolerant of late-comers. This morning's meeting was a bit unusual in that we had a guest speaker. He was giving an encouraging message on how good God was to lead us through so many difficult situations. After our guest finished, Oren decided to take up a love offering for him.

At the close of the service Oren called Susie and me up front, together with all the children, and Marc and Angela. He and several other base leaders laid their hands on us and began to pray a blessing upon us for protection and for opportunities to be used mightily for God's glory. Heartened and encouraged, I looked up and moved to herd my family back to our seats, when I heard the visiting pastor speak out.

"Oren, I feel the Lord wants me to take the love offering you all took for me and give it to this family for their trip." Surprised, I quickly looked over to where he was standing. He didn't know we had any particular need; I'm sure he just figured that any missionary could use a little extra cash on a trip that size.

> God had precisely met the need that morning (plus three bucks extra!).

The secretary finished counting the offering, handed it to the pastor, who in turn passed it over to me. I glanced down (trying not to look too eager) to see what the total came to, and then lifted my head in amazement. It was $343. We all rejoiced together as I shared with everyone how we had been trusting the Lord to provide the last $340 our budget demanded. God had precisely met the need that morning (plus three bucks extra!). This confirmed we were indeed in the center of His will. So with our faith strengthened, God charged us full of confidence into the adventure that lay ahead.[8]

---

8. Hebrews 13:21; I John 5:14-15

Chapter Eight

MIRACLE HEALING IN GUATEMALA

"…and heal those in it who are sick, and say to them, 'The
kingdom of God has come near to you.'" Luke 10:9

"Look, Dad!" My ear tingled with seven-year-old
Ben's excited yell. I glanced to where he was pointing, and
there, running across the road in front of us, was a huge,
scaly iguana.

"What is it?" he asked. "It looks like some humongous
lizard!" My brother, Marc, and I exchanged a smile at his
fairly accurate description of the now illustrious tropical
reptile. I could hear the voices of the girls in the back as
they strained to see:

"Where?" "I don't see it." "What does it look like?"
"Did we pass it already, Dad?" "Couldn't you just back up so
we can look? It will only take a minute." All was quiet for
a second as each gazed out at the thick, bright green trees,
bushes, and vines that surrounded us.

"Hey, Dad, are we in the jungle?" one of the kids asked
in awe. I couldn't help smiling. Guatemala was not quite the
jungle, but it was a lot more fun to see it through their eyes.
No matter how tired and cranky we were by now, I was glad
that we had all been able to come.

We'd been on the road now for six long and exhausting days. Traveling was slow. It had to be—with all five of the children along. Traveling on narrow, bumpy roads behind old diesel trucks that spewed black exhaust didn't make the travel time any faster. Anyway, I was sure we had enough time to meet the outreach participants at the airport in Guatemala City.

The biggest challenge was our lack of Spanish skills, which became evident at the U.S./Mexico border. This was the first time I'd ever tried to cross the border without a translator, so I made sure beforehand that all my papers were in good order. Finally, after many gestures, a few well-placed tips, and a couple hours of waiting for the proper stamps and signatures, we were waved on through. Of course, the border crossing was only the beginning of the journey. After that, I struggled to communicate wherever I stopped to buy gas, food, or purified water. How could I be sure the guy was saying, "Yes, this is purified," and not, "Yes, this is rainwater that I dipped out of my mamcita's wash-bucket"? One hot afternoon we stopped at a little "tienda" (Spanish for "convenience store") to buy some ice-cold pop, very inexpensive in Latin America. We chose the flavor by its color because we couldn't read the labels. Back in the van, my thirsty passengers guzzled their sodas. Marc, who was sitting right beside me, took a swig of his light brown soda – ginger ale possibly? A strange look passed over his face, and he quickly brought the bottle down from his lips.

We had ignorantly bought cheap Mexican beer. Whoops!

"Andy," my disgusted brother choked out, "this is beer!" I sniffed it and took a sip. We had ignorantly bought cheap Mexican beer. Whoops—those two bottles had to go!

After we crossed the Mexico/Guatemala border, the lush green trees with huts hidden in the foliage looked as much like jungle as any pictures I'd seen. Guatemala City was about a day's drive from the border. It looked as if we'd arrive just in time for us to meet the first of our outreach participants at the airport. As we sped along, I noticed one of the road signs had the name of an unfamiliar city written on it. A feeling of weary dread started to work its way through me. What if –?

"Marc, get out the map, would you?" Checking the map, we discovered we had been traveling down the wrong road for at least an hour. With a groan I turned our rig around to back-track all those kilometers. I would definitely be late meeting those guys at the airport.

Shifting uncomfortably in my seat, I checked the rear-view mirror. The van was unusually quiet. We had finally arrived at the place where we had made the wrong turn and were now back on track, straight to Guatemala City. All I could hear was the sound of the engine and the rain which had begun to pour down some time ago. Exhausted from our days of travel, everyone had either fallen asleep or was staring blankly out the window at the wet scenery passing by. Susie and Angela were lying down in the back. Marc sat beside me. All five of the kids sat wedged in the bench seat directly behind mine, where they could see out the windows better. We usually didn't allow the kids to ride without seatbelts. The baby sitting on Gracie's lap like that probably wasn't too safe, but after seven days on the road it didn't seem to matter. Nobody wears seatbelts in Guatemala anyway. I broke the silence with a hopeful word.

"I think it's only about three more hours, guys!" They smiled and their eyes brightened, but they were far too tired to respond very exuberantly. That was fine with me; I was too tired to handle exuberance at the moment. I adjusted my speed to take the next curve carefully.

And that's when it happened… My stomach tightened as I recalled the events of that afternoon. My mind replayed the accident over and over. I could see our travel trailer smashed to bits, with clothes and diapers strewn everywhere, Susie and Angela sloshing through rain and mud to retrieve anything they could from the wreckage. That's when Bill had come, and like an angel from God, he had taken our shocked and muddy crew to his home, where his wife Lupe fed us and offered us a place to sleep.

Suddenly it dawned on me that I had to get a message through to the YWAM base. Not only were we expected to arrive today, but at that very moment the first outreach participant was waiting for me at the airport! The problem was this: the base didn't have a telephone. I decided to try to leave a message at the big Pan-American Hotel in the city, hoping it would be delivered to the base. At this point, what else could I do? When I called I discovered to my amazement that the guy I was supposed to pick up from the airport was already at the hotel. Before I left Arkansas, I had told him that if for some reason I wasn't there to meet him, he should go to the Pan-American Hotel and ask for someone from YWAM. After explaining our predicament, we arranged for him to go in a cab to the YWAM base and to relay the message of our delay. I breathed a sigh of relief as I finished that phone call. God had performed another miracle.

Sleeping in Bill and Lupe's beautiful home that night with my family around me, I felt the arms of God reassuring me that He had us in His hands. Walking through memories of the last 12 years and the Lord's faithfulness to us only increased the peace which had spread over me. In the blackness of night I fell asleep next to Susie, listening to the quiet breathing of our little ones, my heart full of gratitude.

The following week for me was spent talking with officials and filling out forms in an attempt to get the accident cleared up legally. In this too I could see the Lord's hand in having Bill and Lupe help us. Lupe was well known and respected in the community as the one who had worked so hard to bring telephones and a school into the area. She knew all the right people to talk to, the right words to say, and the right forms to fill out. With her assistance, after four days of negotiations and finding all the right officials to sign all the right forms, not only were my driver's license and van returned to me but the other driver's insurance company paid me 3,000 quetzals (equal to 3,000 U.S. dollars) to partially cover the damage.

Susie's week, on the other hand, was spent washing every item of clothing we had. Everything we owned had been completely soaked and soiled. We had brought a small portable washing machine with us to make things more convenient for Susie, and this little wonder was a thrill to Lupe and her maid. They thought it was the most ingenious thing they had ever seen. And at this point, so did Susie! The little spinner-basket spun out load after load of clean clothes, which were hung up to dry on the back fence. With the help of Angela and Lupe's maid, Susie was able to get everything in shape in just a few days. The kids had a blast spending their days playing and catching lizards in the yard behind the house; nearly every day they went swimming at a pool just down the road.

It seemed that every night for the last few years her stomach was in terrible pain.

During the course of our stay, we were given much opportunity to share with Bill and Lupe about our God. About half-way through the week, Susie noticed that Lupe often complained about a stomach problem.

It seemed that every night for the last few years her stomach was in terrible pain. Susie told her that our God heals people and asked if we could pray for her. She responded eagerly. Susie, Marc, and I laid our hands on her and prayed that she be healed.

I must confess that our faith was small and weak but, to our surprise and joy, the next morning Lupe told us that she had been healed. The night before was the first night in years that she had no trouble at all with her stomach, and time would soon prove that she had indeed been totally healed. God had showed Himself mighty yet again. The evening before we left their home to move on, Marc asked her if she would like to receive Jesus as her own Savior and Lord. Her response was a positive "Yes". That night the angels in heaven rejoiced with us.

We left the next morning to complete the journey we had begun two weeks earlier. All of our necessities that had filled the travel trailer before were now packed in plastic garbage bags filling the back half of the van. This left two bucket seats and one bench seat for the nine of us to cram into for the remaining three hour ride to the YWAM base located in the mountains outside of Guatemala City. We didn't hear too many complaints about being crowded, though. We were finally on our way again and the excitement of "getting there" was building in all of us, making these last three hours the longest of all.

We got there in the afternoon and upon our arrival were welcomed with a party. There was a spirit of rejoicing that God had brought us through it all. We had made it! It didn't take us too long to settle into the one small room allotted to our family. Since the room contained only one bunk bed, we used the cushions we had salvaged from the wrecked travel trailer for beds. At night we'd spread them out on the floor to sleep on, and in the day we'd fold and stack them to make a couch for "day-time lounging."

Of course the kids didn't want to stay in the room much anyway, especially since there was a swimming pool on the grounds right behind where we were staying! We bought large woven baskets to put our clothes in. Since we had packed directly into the travel-trailer's drawers, we didn't have any suitcases along. This would surely make for interesting travel arrangements on the return trip home!

The outreach participants had arrived and were raring to go. We started out with tried-and-true Bible distribution. This was always an effective ministry tool in which any level of language skills would be sufficient. Getting God's Word into the hands of the people is an important step in evangelizing a nation. With Angela to help watch our children, it was fun to have Susie and sometimes the older kids along to see and experience it all firsthand.

A highlight of the outreach was the day we visited the orphanage. Everyone, even Gracie and Ben, pitched in to paint buildings, mend the children's clothes, and clean various facilities. A couple of guys even found a rusty old lawnmower and decided to mow the grass. What a classic picture it made. Several young guys, engineering majors in college, all gathered around the ancient piece of machinery tinkering with it until finally they fixed it (at least temporarily) with an old horseshoe nail. Then they triumphantly cut the grass. Serving "the least of these" had never been so satisfying.

There was a great need for more laborers in the harvest field. My vision was to help others see the need and do something about it. The young people would come for a few weeks to serve, and they would leave, never to be the same again. God imparted something to them that would forever be a part of the way they'd live.

I loved the people of Guatemala and was excited about all the Lord was doing in this country, changing it around for His glory. My wife and kids already loved it also, having adjusted easily to all the different changes. Nevertheless, as our two months there went by, and we sought the Lord for His direction concerning a permanent move, Susie and I both felt strongly that the answer was, "No. Go back to

Arkansas and plant roots."

It seemed crazy. We liked it here and were ready to stay. Plant roots? What sort of real missionary is going to plant roots in the United States?

However, I knew better. A real missionary is one whose heart and life are committed to fulfilling God's purposes for the world,[1] and who is obedient to God's direction no matter what it is.[2] It seemed difficult for a zealous, go-to-the-nations-type missionary like me to obey God's direction to stay rather than go, but Susie and I knew for certain that we could trust God to use us most effectively as we obeyed Him. Returning to Elm Springs, I wondered if God was going to give us the home He had promised to Susie years earlier while we were planting roots. Who knew? But we would plant roots, and we would do so wherever He led us.

1. II Peter 3:9 2. Psalm 40:8; Matthew 7:21; Mark 3:35

Chapter Nine

THE LETTER WITH THE FACTS

"For it is superfluous for me to write to you about this
ministry to the saints; for I know your readiness..."
II Corinthians 9:1,2a

Looking up from my Bible, I stretched and shifted my
position, various body parts tingling from my prolonged
recline with only a sleeping bag and thin mat between
myself and the hard concrete floor. Glancing quickly
around, I didn't take long to survey my surroundings: dull,
rough cement walls and floor, few screenless windows and
a door. The view from the windows didn't do a whole lot
to thrill the soul either: gray, crowded streets; thick smog;
newly constructed cement buildings amid blackened heaps
of rubble. This was Mexico City.

Several of us from YWAM Elm Springs had come to
join the thousands of YWAMers from around the world to
evangelize during the 1986 World Cup Soccer Games held
in Mexico that muggy June. Working together we were able
to reach the many thousands present for the games through
street evangelism, puppet shows, open-air preaching, and
whatever other method presented itself. Having survived
a devastating earthquake only weeks before the games, the
hearts of many Mexicans were open, tragedy bringing them
to a realization of their need for God.

I rested that hot Sunday afternoon in my room (on the fourth floor of the half-finished Nazarene hospital where I was living with 250 other YWAMers), reading my Bible and spending a few moments alone with God. As I was reading, a verse seemed to "jump out at me." Jesus said:

"And no one puts new wine into old wineskins; otherwise the wine will burst the skins, and the wine is lost, and the skins as well; but one puts new wine into fresh wineskins." Mark 2:22.

It seemed the Lord was speaking to me through this Scripture.

"Andy," He said, "you've got an old YWAMer's heart like that old wineskin. Changes are coming, and you need a fresh heart if I'm going to be able to pour new things into it." I couldn't know what this was to mean in the next months, but I did know the Lord was preparing me for something. All I could do was open my heart and allow Him to make it new.

At 5:00 a.m. all was quiet but for the grating beep of my alarm clock which I quickly silenced. In the dim light of my room I quietly put on my clothes, gently opened the door, and tip-toed down the three flights of concrete stairs and out. I found myself in the still, bus-lined street outside the building I had called "home" for the past two weeks. Today I would be flying back to the States, so in the cool of the early morning I hurried to carry out the plan I had been scheming for several days now.

I missed Susie terribly this trip. I wished she could have come, but with our newest family member still quite small, it had been impossible. In March another son, Joseph, had been born to us. After three girls in a row, little Joey came a pleasant surprise to us all. Ben was especially pleased, finally not quite so outnumbered by the girls. I couldn't wait to get home to them all, knowing how excited they'd be over the little Mexican souvenirs I'd picked up for them. With the presents bought and packed, there was only one thing left to do.

I arrived at the small store, the first customer of the day. The heavy scent of flowers filled the warm air in the flower shop. Days earlier I had discovered that they sold flowers at a very low price; I had been plotting my surprise ever since. I walked over to the lady and somehow communicated my desire to buy some roses for my wife. The thrilled shopkeeper quickly showed me to the freshly cut roses. I then proceeded to purchase not one dozen or even two dozen, but twelve dozen roses–a dozen for each year we had been married. I chose red, yellow, pink, white, and deep purple roses–fully a hundred and forty-four of them–and watched with a smile as the lady carefully wrapped and boxed them for me. What a bargain I was getting: 12 dozen roses for less than $20, and a gift my wife could never forget.

Hours later I was homeward bound, the large box of blossoms tucked between my knees as my carry-on for the plane ride. I gratefully thanked the Lord for the sympathetic customs official who had given me little trouble in carrying them across the border. A stewardess walked by, sniffing the air with a puzzled look on her face. Where did that scent come from? She smiled as did several other travelers realizing the box contained flowers. Probably for a special occasion. Yes, indeed.

Susie met me at the airport in Tulsa, Oklahoma. Since it was about two hours from home, we decided to rent a hotel room for the night and drive back the next day. I waited until the perfect moment.

When we arrived at the hotel, Susie sat down to nurse the baby while I unloaded the car. Since she was occupied, it was easy to slip the box into the bathroom. I locked the door, and arranged the flowers in a large vase that I had borrowed from the front desk. Susie tucked the sleeping baby into bed and came near the bathroom to help with the unpacking. I stepped out, shut the door and covered Susie's eyes.

"Andy, what...?"

"I brought you a surprise," I explained as I led her to a chair. "Now sit right there, and keep your eyes covered."

She complied, only teasing me by peeking through the cracks in her fingers.

"No peeking!" I said as I headed for the hidden flowers. When I returned with the huge bouquet, the still fresh flowers permeated the air with their fragrance. Susie still had her eyes covered, so I told her to take a deep breath and guess what I brought her.

"Oh, it's a rose," she said with delight. Then I uncovered her eyes, and gleefully watched her face transform into an expression I'll never forget. Her giddy smile and tight squeeze warmed my heart. She was worth more than 10,000 roses.

Her giddy smile and tight squeeze warmed my heart. She was worth more than 10,000 roses.

Changes were to come that fall, especially in the area of our YWAM base's financial policy. Whereas before the housing was provided for staff, now because of the growth of the ministry and increase in staff numbers, staff would be required to help carry the financial load of paying monthly rent and utilities. We were already very financially stretched, but always had been able to take heart in the fact that we did have a place to stay (crowded though it was) and always had our meals at the brooder. Our children were receiving a good education at no cost as well. We had our basic needs met and were content and thankful. But now, the news of these additional fees came as quite a blow to us. We simply did not have the resources to pay. It took all the mustering of our meager faith to push away the whispers in our hearts saying, "Here we are giving our lives to serve this ministry for no salary whatsoever, and now we're going to have to pay to do it as well."

The weeks went by and we continued battling the discouragement threatening to defeat us. What could I do? We had given up everything to follow God's call on our family. We had obeyed His direction in coming to serve this ministry. We had trusted Him with every detail of our lives for ten years now and had truly seen Him prove Himself faithful time and again. We had been obedient, giving to the church of God, challenging them with vision, serving and loving them, and also making our needs known to them. As far as I could see, we had done all that God had asked of us, not without some failings, but always sincerely and with a heart to do His will. And now, not only were our costs of basic living increasing by a substantial amount, but our support seemed to be drying up. The cruel facts were that we could not afford to work with YWAM any longer.

"What can I do, Lord? I've done all I know to do; You promised in the woodshop years ago that You'd show me a better way if I'd trust You. Does financial support-raising through friendship building really work, or have I done it all wrong?

My questions were honest and coming from a heart that sincerely wanted to serve Him...but what about the money?

About this time, a man I had met in Wisconsin called me with an incredible offer. He had a retreat center and wanted to use it to develop a program to train young missionaries for Africa. Would I consider coming and heading up the program? We would be given a house to live in and, although we would need to raise funds for the ministry, I personally would be paid a salary. I could develop the training program as I pleased, the only stipulation being that the missionaries would be sent to Africa.

This opportunity sounded tremendously appealing to our discouraged, weary souls. Our money problem would be taken care of, we'd have a larger house for our family, and we'd still be able to serve the Lord full-time in missions work, doing the very thing our hearts wanted to do. It truly did seem that a "spiritual" way out of our present struggle had come.

But as Susie and I prayed about the possibility of undertaking this project, I realized that there was no way we could pack up and leave while things were still unsettled.

"Susie," I said, "we've got to weather this storm. We can't just take off because things seem impossible right now. We've got to keep doing the last thing the Lord told us to do. Maybe God does want us to accept this offer, and if He does, we can be certain that He will lead us. If we are going to leave and start something new, God will have to tell us to go as clearly as He told us to come here. We just can't take things into our own hands right now." So I called the man in Wisconsin, telling him that at this time we would not be able to join him in his project, but if in six months the offer still stood, he could call again. He never did.

My questions were honest and coming from a heart that sincerely wanted to serve Him... but what about the money?

We continued to seek God, pleading for His direction and provision. As we did, we felt that we should write another letter to all the people who received our newsletter. We both struggled with this.

"Lord, we already did that and it didn't work," Susie prayed, a bit discouraged.

"Write another one anyway," she felt the Lord reply, "Don't worry; it will work." We felt a bit like Peter when he was all tired and discouraged after fishing all night, catching nothing. Then Jesus called out and told him to throw his net out on the other side of the boat just one more time.

So, with pen and legal pad in hand, we began to write, leaving out none of the facts. We received no regular salary for our labor. Due to the tremendous growth of our staff, it was a financial impossibility for the training base to provide food and housing for all personnel and our families. Our cost of living would therefore increase dramatically. Our circumstances were such that we could continue serving full-time with YWAM only if we raised enough financial support to sustain our family's needs. Looking up from the scrawled yellow sheet, I pondered what to say next, then continued with the letter:

"Honestly, when we first faced the facts of how much financial support we would have to raise in order to fully cover our expenses, it was a bit discouraging. The staggering figure of $1800 a month sent us to our knees. There, the Lord assured us in the still, and quiet, but matter-of-fact way of His Spirit that He would move on hearts of committed friends and missions-minded churches to support us as we continued to labor for His Kingdom.

"Here's the matter laid before you. We need friends to commit themselves to monthly support of $100, $50, $30 or whatever they can send. Please ask the Lord if He would allow you to be a part of our ministry at this time by supporting us monthly during the coming year. Then, please take a few minutes to fill out the enclosed card and mail it back to us. We need your response as soon as possible. I'll be in touch with you if I don't hear from you.

"Thank you so much for hearing our hearts. We're deeply grateful for you, and look forward to hearing from you. Once again, I want to remind you that unless our monthly support needs are met, we will reevaluate where God would have us serve."

I signed my name and wearily sat back in my chair for

a minute. Unwelcome thoughts began to storm my mind. What would people think? Here we were, point-blank asking for money. My imagination could just hear their questions and comments: "He must not be in God's will," or "What kind of organization does he work for anyway? No salary! That's crazy," or " Why doesn't he just go to work and get a real job?" Yet I knew that this was a real job. Working with all my might to help get the gospel out to the millions who don't have Jesus definitely was a job that had to be done. Who would take my place if I quit? I became more determined than ever to press on.

Susie "edited" the letter, we printed it out on some beautiful stationery given to us by a friend, and stuffed each envelope with a letter, response card, and return envelope for their convenience. After addressing and stamping each letter, I took a deep breath. They were ready to mail. Should I really do it?

God didn't think of us as "beggars" at all.

Susie and I sat in the parking lot of a grocery store, anointing each letter with oil and praying, in faith, that the oil of the Holy Spirit would touch people's hearts as they read our letter. We didn't want to offend anyone by asking for money, but at the same time we knew that it was God's specific direction for us, fully supported by His Word.

A few weeks passed and letters began to appear more frequently in our mailbox. Many were simple notes of encouragement along with a commitment to stand with us. It seemed that quite a few of my friends had no idea of our financial position: that we received no salary. In fact, many wondered why I had never written before and were glad I had, to let them know of the situation. As a result, we found we did have true friends who had never intended to let us go without what we needed to continue our missionary service to God. The good response we got was not merely monthly support, but confirmation that we were indeed hearing God's voice and doing His will. Our financial trial was far from being over, but in the midst of the struggle we had received blessing, hope, and encouragement from God's people "sending us on our way."[1] God didn't think of us as "beggars" at all. We were His laborers worthy of our wages.[2]

*   *   *

One evening shortly after that realization, I looked around the table as we sat in the kitchen eating our supper, a soup of leftovers Susie had somehow made delicious. The small table was covered with bowls, cups of water, packages of crackers, plates sporting mutilated sticks of margarine, and an abundance of elbows. Then one of the kids asked for some ice as their soup was too hot. Susie got up from where she had been spooning mush into baby Joey's half-toothed mouth because her chair was right in front of the refrigerator. Then a wail went up in our midst! Jessica got a glass of water dumped in her lap. She was crying because it wasn't her fault, but the accidental result of a neighboring elbow from when Susie stood to access the refrigerator. One of the older kids turned to help, grabbing a crumpled towel from the counter directly behind her chair. Sniffling and damp, Jessica asked for a new glass of water. With a sigh I reached for her cup and turned in my seat to the sink that was behind me. I could get her drink without ever leaving my chair — our kitchen was so crowded. It was impossible to walk around the table with everyone seated. During the meal we generally served the food and then put the serving bowls back on the counter or stove to conserve as much of the limited table space as possible for the more frequently used items.

"Lord," I thought for the hundredth time, "we have got to have more space. We are getting so crowded! Please provide something bigger for us." One kid squeezed past

1. III John 6 2. Luke 10:7

another's chair in attempt to leave the table. I'd been house-hunting a lot lately but hadn't found anything yet. We'd have to do something soon, though.

Susie was pregnant again. The revelation came as a surprise to us all. Although I loved all my kids and was glad to have another, I wasn't sure where we'd put this new one. We already had the bedrooms packed to capacity and even had to have one of our daughters sleep on the living room couch every night. I guessed when the new baby was born, the "old" baby, Joey, not even two yet, could move out of the crib and into the living room with Jessica. We would simply have to make room. What about God's promise to Susie of a home? With the kids getting older and more numerous, I didn't know how much longer we could wait around for the Lord's "promise."

I didn't know how much longer we could wait around for the Lord's "promise."

For a few weeks I looked at houses, contemplated loans, and did everything I could to move us into something different, but things did not seem to come together. One night I opened my eyes, suddenly wide-awake. Everything was still dark and quiet. I glanced over to the small clock I kept on the windowsill by my bed: it was about 4:00 a.m. I lay there for a minute and then, knowing the Lord wanted to speak to me, crawled out of the tangled covers and went to the kitchen table and sat down with my Bible. I took my time to wander through the pages reviewing the different passages I had been studying lately. As I read and pondered the counsel and teaching concerning financial stewardship that the Lord had brought my way in recent months; I knew it was not the Lord's highest for me to take out a bank loan to buy a house.[3] I was challenged again to trust Him for His supernatural provision:

"I've promised your family a home. If you'll trust me

---

3. Proverbs 10:22

and wait, I'll do something greater than all you can ask or think."

Was this God, or just my own middle-of-the-night imagination? I wrestled with this thought, truly wanting to please God, but balking at the thought of waiting even longer for our situation to be eased. Finally, a couple of hours later, I let go of my own attempts to "help" God meet our need for a house. Placing our predicament wholly in His hands once again, I lifted my heart, yielding my own means of solving the problem.

"Father," I prayed, "if we have to live in tents we'll still trust you. We know that You will always be faithful to Your word."[4] I couldn't help hoping, though, that it really wasn't a tent the Lord had in store for us. I poured a cup of coffee to take to Susie, wanting her to wake up so I could discuss with her what the Lord had revealed, before the mobile home exploded with busy children.

---

4. Hebrews 6:13-20

Chapter Ten

THE OLD BLUE VAN IS DEAD

"Delight yourself in the Lord; And He will give you the desires of your heart." Psalms 37:4

I looked down at the words I had jotted down on my piece of scratch paper, "FINANCIAL FOCUS." I was working on the rough draft of our newsletter to send to Bruce and Mary Scott. They had been faithfully blessing us for years now by helping us send out a professional-looking newsletter every two months. This "financial focus" heading always made me stop and think, "What are our true needs right now?" Never would I want to misuse the Lord's newsletter or the generosity of our friends to fulfill my own selfish "wants." Of course, this usually wasn't the temptation. The problem most of the time was in deciding which of our many legitimate needs to present. After thinking a moment longer I began to write, laying out as briefly and concisely as possible the nature of our financial needs at this point:

1. $500 needed for the cost of having the baby at home (midwife and supplies)
2. A dependable replacement vehicle that will seat-belt nine of us as a family. Our eleven-year-old Ford van is worn out!

These two needs really were the most urgent of all. Our seventh baby[1] was due in about a month now. Having

---

1. Psalm 107:41-42

a home birth did decrease the expenses, but it still cost quite a bit to have a baby. Besides, Susie had been sick for this entire pregnancy, even to the point of having to go to the hospital a few months earlier. All we could do was pray that this delivery would be smooth and safe for both Susie and the little one. And it was also true that our blue van really was shot, and the need for a new vehicle was getting desperate. It was nearly November and the weather was starting to get pretty chilly. With no heater as well as major transmission problems, I didn't want Susie to drive the van anymore. It just wasn't safe. But there wasn't much I could do about it. We'd simply have to trust and wait patiently for the provision of the Lord.

Two weeks later I sat at my desk in the office at the base, busily sorting through all the papers and work that were my responsibility. It was just another day in the office. I glanced at the clock. It was about 10:00 a.m. My phone rang–not anything to get excited over at my desk. I answered, and on the other end of the line was a businessman, wanting to know how everything was going for us. Well, honestly, we were being pretty stretched these days. No point going into details, I guessed. Eventually the conversation shifted just a bit.

"I noticed in your last newsletter that you said your old blue van's about worn out," he casually mentioned.

"Yeah, well, it's barely working. The transmission keeps slipping, and also the heater's busted, so it'll be pretty cold in there this winter. I won't even let Susie drive it anymore." I hoped I didn't sound too discouraged. So many problems seemed to be mounting: the expense of a new baby, Susie's poor health, our cramped quarters, broken transportation. When would the breakthrough come?

"Andy," my friend interrupted my weary thoughts, "we'd like to help you get another vehicle. What kind are you needing?" I was astounded. Could he be saying what I thought he was saying? I replied somewhat tentatively,

"I suppose we'd have to get something that will seat-belt nine people. The only two vehicles I can think of that are that big are another van or a GMC Suburban."

"What is it that you like, Andy?"

What did I like? I didn't even think that way anymore. I took either what people gave me or what I could afford–which wasn't much. But here he was asking, not what was cheapest, but what we really needed and wanted.

He continued, "Why don't you go out shopping and take a look. Just two stipulations: it's got to be under 30,000 miles and also less than two years old." My head spun. Surely the man knew a vehicle that big and in that good of condition would cost thousands. Could I dare hope that? Well, hey, Susie and I were going out "car-shopping" and were going to enjoy it whether I had understood my friend correctly or not. Maybe, just maybe, the sunlight was about to break through the discouraging clouds of our storm.

> But here he was asking, not what was cheapest, but what we really needed and wanted.

We went from dealership to dealership looking at everything that could fit us all. Finally, after checking all the options, we boiled it down to our two top choices: a Ford XLT van, and a GMC Suburban. Both were nice, comfortable, in excellent condition, but also very expensive. The Suburban really was the one I had my eye on. Brown tones, stylish, roomy interior, 6.2 liter diesel engine, lots of little extras–everything we needed, and just what I liked. It would be great for trips to Mexico too. The only problem was that, even though I knew we could bargain them down a lot, I didn't know if my friend could possibly be expecting me to come up with something priced so high.

But, I remembered that he had told me to look for an adequate vehicle and let him know what I found. So I guessed I'd better call and tell him what I found. Besides, what was the worst thing that could happen? He could say, "Andy, I'm sorry. You completely misunderstood me; that's much too expensive. Let me help you find something cheaper." Well I'd feel pretty dumb, but I'd get over it.

I rummaged through the pile of junk on my desk in the corner of our small trailer's living room, looking for his phone number. Finding it, I held my breath as I dialed. OK, this was it. Lord, help me be normal!

My friend answered. We conversed for a few minutes, touching on all the ordinary greetings and commonplace news that came to mind. As graciously as possible I brought up the fact that I had been searching the local car lots for the past few weeks and had a couple of great finds. He seemed excited that I had found something so quickly and was eager to hear about it, so I launched into the merits of each finally ending with, "I think that, comparing the two, the Suburban is the best deal, will suit our needs the best, and will last the longest." I'd had my say, and now I knew the big question was about to come.

"Well, Andy, how much is it?" I gulped and told him. To my relief, he didn't seem too shocked after all, just said, "I'll bet we can get it for a lot less than that. Why don't you go ahead and start working on a deal?"

So the negotiations began. Going back to look at the Suburban a second time was a sure sign to the salesman that I was definitely interested. Susie and I took it for a test drive and knew this was exactly what we had been looking for. The question was, how would we get the price down to something affordable? Even with the small allowance for trading in our old van, there would still be a few thousand dollars difference between the taking price and the asking price of $17,000. I'd have to wait it out for a while before

I made our final bid. There was still hope I could work the price down a bit more.

Susie's due date was now past, leaving her not only huge but miserable with waiting for our newest family member to escape. We were all relieved when, on the 4th of December, Susie went into labor. The labor seemed to go on forever until finally, mid-morning on the 5th, Nicholas Lee took his place as the youngest of the Huddleston crew. (To our amusement, a few days later we discovered that we had named him "Nicholas" without even realizing that he was born on St. Nicholas' Day!) Susie was exhausted but blissful and, despite a few scary complications, was soon resting peacefully in her bed with our new son in her arms. Our six other children quickly nosed their way into the small room to quietly look at their new baby brother.

Since it was now early December, I knew most people were out shopping for Christmas, not cars. I figured it would be to my advantage to make my best offer on the Suburban now. I called Jim, the salesman I had been dealing with, and made my offer. His response? No way! My offer, even with the old van included, was much too low. I waited a few more days and called back with my absolute final offer. If he didn't take it, that was it. Jim was still extremely doubtful, but he agreed to submit it to his managers as the final decision was not his to make. I gave him my number to call me if the deal went through.

Less than 15 minutes later our phone rang. I moved to answer it and was surprised when I heard the salesman's voice so soon: "Believe it or not, the management accepted your offer. You can come get the Suburban tomorrow at about noon and pay your balance on Friday." Dazed, I thanked him and hung up. I sat back for a minute, then picked up the phone back up and called the man who had so generously offered to buy us this Suburban. Both of us were excited that the Lord had arranged for us to get a fair price. The very next day, I drove the Suburban home, thoroughly enjoying the strength of the diesel engine, the smooth way the power-steering guided the big vehicle through traffic, the warmth of the heater, and the soft support of the driver's seat. As I played with the speaker system for the radio, I felt overwhelmed with the goodness of the Lord. He had promised to meet our needs, but this truly was more than I could ever have asked or even dreamed of.[2]

That afternoon I sat with my friend in the Suburban he had just bought for us and our ministry. Gratitude choking me up a bit, I asked him if he'd be willing to lead us in prayer, committing this vehicle and its use to the Lord and the advancement of His kingdom. We prayed and after we were through, he looked up and said,

"Andy, I've been watching you and Susie for several years now, and I know you would keep serving God whether you had a good vehicle or not." Wiping a tear from his eye, he continued, "If you knew what my wife and I went through in the early days of our business, you would understand that we know what it's like to drive beat-up cars, shop flea markets, and spend the little we did have to pay the doctors' bills. I'm so glad I can be a part of the answer to your family's need." It sure felt like Christmas for Susie and me—our trials were passing, a new baby and a newer vehicle. It's seemed the "day of the Lord" was coming for us and we welcomed it.

*   *   *

One day soon after Christmas, with my arms filled with the brittle greenery, I made my way out the small door of

---

our mobile home. I commanded one of my little helpers out of the way to clear the path for my ceremonial dumping of this year's Christmas tree on the ground next to the small porch outside. We could never seem to put up with this particular symbol of the season's festivities very long after Christmas Day, since it occupied so much of our precious living space.

I knew this space would only shrink as the children grew bigger, but all I could really do was trust and wait for the Lord; He knew our circumstances and had promised to take care of us. Besides, I was weary of trying to change things in my own strength.

We kept looking in the area for a house suitable to our needs but really couldn't come up with anything. I called Don, our pastor and friend. He suggested that we begin looking for a piece of land rather than a house, because the size of our family presented a unique need. We could then build a house that would suit our requirements perfectly. He also advised that we look for a piece of property located on a paved road, with full accessibility to city water and other utilities to make the house easier to sell if the Lord ever moved us on. We considered his wise counsel and started hunting.

We spent many hours scouring the surrounding countryside for the available building lots. Since Elm Springs was pretty much rural, there seemed to be acres and acres of vacant land wherever we went. The reality was that the various landowners were farmers who weren't yet ready to sell. We looked and looked, and could not find one piece of suitable property available to even dream of buying.

In the meantime, though, it gave Susie and me an escape tactic when the hectic pace of nine people (plus neighbors) roaring around in our "tin can" mobile home became too much. We could disappear for a couple hours leaving the younger children under the care of the older ones, our excuse being "We're going to look for a piece of land by faith." But even with all our hunting we still turned up empty-handed; there was simply nothing to be found.

Then one evening, when I returned from my day in the base's office, Susie met me with some big news.

"Guess what, Andy?! I found a 'For Sale' sign in that cow pasture out there just behind the base!" I tried to smother my doubt of her words. We had been past that field countless times, and the owner had never shown any intention of selling. Susie must have seen something else. But no, she said she had gotten frustrated with our jammed quarters that morning, packed up the two little boys and gone for a drive. Passing by the field she saw a real estate sign advertising its availability.

Still having a hard time believing her, we got into the Suburban and drove the short distance to the field. There was no sign to be seen–just cows munching away at the grass. I only half-listened to Susie's insistence that she really had seen the sign there that morning, thinking with amusement that perhaps the strain had become a bit too much for her.

Not feeling too disappointed because I hadn't really expected anything in the first place, I drove back to the base and parked beside our mobile home. As soon as we got back, Susie insisted that I call the real estate company whose name she was sure she had seen. I did–and found out that she was right. It was for sale! Well! Maybe Susie hadn't lost her sanity after all!

We went back to check out the piece of land again, this time taking a closer look. The pasture, surrounded by a barbed-wire fence, adjoined the small subdivision located directly behind the base. The street was fully paved and was connected to the narrow highway that ran through Elm Springs. We had driven through the quiet neighborhood a number of times, but nothing had been available. This two-acre strip of field was right in line with the subdivision and would easily be accessible to water lines as well as electricity and natural gas. By road it was only a little more than a mile from the base. And since the neighborhood was right behind the base's property line, it was only a five minute walk across a field to the base. It was ideal. We stood outside of our Suburban just looking for several minutes.

I felt Susie grab my arm as she pointed to a weedy spot in the pasture.

"Look, Andy! Over there!" I didn't see anything, so I looked closer. Wait! What was that laying on the ground? I began to laugh. It was the "For Sale" sign Susie had seen, probably knocked over by some itchy cow using it as a scratching post.

"Maybe the Lord had the cow knock it down so nobody else would see it and buy it before we got a chance!" she said with a poke.

I called Don the next day to tell him that we'd finally found a piece of land. He came over the next afternoon to look at it with me, agreeing that it really was a fine plot. What was more, he personally knew the man who operated that particular real estate company and was sure he could get a good deal. He said he'd start working on a deal right away. He wanted to buy it for us. Wow!

We were going to build a house! The thought was more than I could realistically imagine.

A few weeks later, carefully dodging the "cow pies," I walked over the plot of land God had given us to call our own. I marveled at the thought. We were still living in the mobile home of course, but now that we had this piece of property, the immense reality of what the Lord certainly wanted us to do next hit me. We were going to build a house! The thought was more than I could realistically imagine. Sure, I had done my share of carpentry and construction over the years, but to personally build a house from start to finish...? I tramped through the tall weeds over to where Jonathan, a friend from church who happened to be a contractor, was surveying the land. He was looking for the best place to build. Looking up from his surveying instrument he asked in an almost teasing manner,

"So, Andy, do you have your blueprints yet?" I paused, chuckling at the thought of the crazy story I was going to get to tell.

Several months earlier Susie and I had gone to Kansas City to attend a conference, and there met with another contractor friend who was building a subdivision on the outskirts of the city. He took us for the grand tour, showing us the different styles of houses he'd built. Knowing the size of our family and our present cramped situation, he pointed to one of the houses saying,

"Look over there. That's the house you need." It was a huge, beautiful house, the different angles of the roof creating a modern homey look.

I jokingly turned to the guy and said, "Got an extra set of those house plans you want to give us?!"

Unexpectedly his reply was, "Actually, I do have an extra set at the office if you want to drop by and get them now." I wasn't sure what to say; I had just been kidding. Oh, well, might as well take them.

We returned from our trip and stowed the set of blueprints in an obscure corner with a laugh. Come on! As if we were going to build a house, especially such a big, nice one like that! What a joke. We didn't even seriously consider it at the time.

The Lord must have been laughing down at us all along, for now the joke was on us, and a wonderful joke it really was! With a little revision those blueprints were just what we needed, bypassing weeks of often frustrating, not to mention expensive, labor. God had begun the preparations long ago without even bothering to tell us what was going on.

Now, as I looked across the bare field with its few trees and the pond on the adjoining property, my gratitude was colored by the overwhelming feeling of just beginning.

It would take thousands of dollars and months of labor before a real house would stand on the place where the toe of my boot was now digging as I kicked at the rocky soil. Right now it was just a bare field, great one though it was, and a big dream. It would take a miracle–a real one from God.

Chapter Eleven

MIRACLE HOUSE—GOD, BUILDER OF ALL THINGS

"For every house is by someone, but the builder of all things is God." Hebrews 3:4

Staring thoughtfully over Don's shoulder at the bright colored ponchos and sombreros decorating the walls of the small cafe where we sat, I tried to put my confused thoughts in order so I could finish what I had been trying to say. "I just don't know, Don."

He glanced up from his plate of enchiladas to listen as I struggled through this next lesson in placing my trust in God alone.

"It's just that Jesus talked in Luke about how ridiculous it is for someone to start building without calculating the cost to see if he had enough to finish.[1] Right now we don't have the money to complete this house if we start it. Is it foolish for us to do this? I just don't know...".

It was now June, and I had already taken the necessary steps to begin construction but I wasn't in so deep that it would be impossible to pull out if I decided I needed to. I had cleared the land and taken a few months off from my work with YWAM to pour my time fully into this project. I had sent out a letter to all of my friends and supporters to let them know what was going on and to ask them to pray about helping us with any monetary gifts, donation of supplies, or

1. Luke 14:28-30

their own skills. I knew one thing. This was definitely not something I could do alone. My friends responded eagerly, and with one large gift of $10,000 and many smaller gifts coming to nearly $4,000, we had a total of $14,000 to begin working–nearly enough to get the house framed and roofed. Then came the second thoughts. Should I still go for it while lacking the thousands of dollars to complete what I'd begun? Was it faith or folly?

Don, whose counsel I had sought on countless other occasions in the years I'd known him, put down his fork and with conviction in his voice said, "Andy, with the evidence of what God has already done as confirmation of what you believe His will to be, you can begin this with confidence that God will finish it. If you are faithful, God will finish it." Furthermore, he told me that the church volunteered to send out five building-update newsletters during the next few months in order that we could keep everyone informed of our progress and needs; we needed only to provide photos and a rough draft for each letter. Forgetting we were still in the cafe, I took a deep, resolute breath of the stale, cigarette smoke-filled air, only to wish I hadn't inhaled quite so deeply! So there was my answer. I was going to "arise and build" (the theme from Nehemiah 2:18 I had chosen for the appeal letter I'd just sent out), putting my faith in God to help me finish the project He seemed to be starting for me. I realized that I actually had counted the cost, as Jesus had said, and that the real issue was, as always, faith.

That same week we began. I hired a backhoe to come in and dig the footings and within a week, the concrete footings were poured and the blocks were laid. Several staff guys from the base came to help spread the gravel, and then we were ready to pour the foundation. The following Saturday a group of men from our church came and poured the cement slab. With the foundation and slab of the floor now finished, it was time to seriously begin building.

My heart was blessed to see all the people who came to give of their time and labor to help me.[2] People wanted to help us. One long-time friend and war veteran, Charles, told me months before we were even planning to build that if we ever did build a house, he wanted to help us. Unfortunately he was in Guatemala when the time actually came that we really needed help to get things done. Even as far away as he was, I decided to call him. At this time I remembered an encouraging scripture verse:

> "He will also lift up a standard to the nations a far off; And will *whistle* for it from the ends of the earth; and behold, it will come with speed swiftly." Isaiah 5:26

The picture that popped into my mind was the scene of my grandfather calling his farm animals from the fields to feed them. Could God be calling others to help us? We'll wait and see.

"Howdy, Charles! We're ready to go. The slab's been poured, and it's time to start framing the house!" He didn't hesitate a moment.

"Yup, I'll be there in a week," he responded in his characteristic back-hills drawl. And sure enough, a week later he was knocking at our mobile home's door, the joy of the Lord beaming through his wide grin. He was rarin' to go (never mind that he had just hitchhiked from Guatemala). He worked with me for eight weeks straight, putting in the long hours *just because he loved us* and wanted to help. In addition to his help and the help of our eleven-year-old

---

2. Zechariah 10:8

Ben, we also had help from people at the base, church youth groups, my brother and sisters, friends I hadn't seen in years and people I'd never even met before. They gave their help for a few hours, a few days, or sometimes a few weeks, blessing us with their eager hearts to serve. It was barely believable, and all I could do was praise the Lord for the faithful and giving hearts of His people.

The heat of the summer grew more intense as June flew by and July began. The house was nearly "in the dry," that is, completely framed and roofed. The Lord had already, in a special way, provided shingles to roof the house. Hail had ruined the roofs of a few houses in the area, so when a friend who was re-shingling his house discovered that he had a lot of leftover shingles, he gave us the surplus. It turned out to be enough to shingle our entire roof. Now the biggest thing that remained in order to complete this first phase of building was to install the windows and doors. The problem was we were out of money.

The problem was: we were out of money.

The salesman came and measured all the windows in order to give me an estimate. I winced as he told me what it would cost.

"Well, it looks like it's going to be around $2,400." I just closed my eyes as he continued to tell me I'd need to order them soon too, if I were to get them in time. He'd come back in a few days to take the order.

The night before the salesman was going to come I took Susie aside and told her to write the last check to pay all the bills we had accumulated in building so far. I knew when that was done our balance would be pretty close to $0.00. I could only wait and trust my God.

Early the next morning I drove out to the building site, and was surprised to find someone already there before me. Rick, a friend from church, was standing near his green pickup truck parked in the driveway. I got out to greet him.

"Hey, Rick! What are you up to this morning?"

"I came to help you for a couple of days," he replied. That was great! He was a skilled worker and a lot of fun to work with besides. We chatted for a few minutes, and I showed him the progress we'd made on the house over the last few weeks. As we walked along he suddenly stopped as if he had just remembered something.

"Say, I was at a prayer meeting this morning and one of the men there gave me an envelope to give to you. Here." He handed me a sealed, blank envelope.

I opened it up right away. My jaw went slack. In the envelope was $2,400, the very amount I needed that morning to order the necessary windows and doors. I had told no one of the need, and out of the blue someone had felt impressed to give the exact amount we needed on the exact morning we needed it. I stood amazed. I knew God would eventually provide for the windows and doors. But, somewhere in the back of my mind, I expected to have to "do without" for a while, struggling and waiting for God's provision. I had never before witnessed one supernatural provision after another quite like this. And there was more to come.

The next morning, I arrived at the house early to have a little time alone with the Lord before the day got into full swing. Kicking aside some of the debris covering the cement, I made a place for myself to stand in what would soon be our living room. Tools, materials, and sawdust were scattered over the floor. The walls separating the rooms were still just framed, making it easy to "walk through the walls." In a few days Steve Collier, my friend from Kentucky, would be coming with his two sons to wire the house for electricity. About the same time the plumber, who was hired by another friend who had volunteered to take care of the plumbing, would be coming to put in all the necessary pipes. Things were really moving quickly and a lot was getting done. The house seemed massive, with several bedrooms, spacious living areas, and a large kitchen and dining room. A sense of awe enveloped me as I stood there looking at the miracle happening around me. Emotion welling up inside, I lifted my face to voice the question that had been forming in my heart for some time now.

"Lord, how?" I entreated. "How can you give us this huge, beautiful home when I've seen with my own eyes people living in squalor with only bits of cardboard and tin to keep the rain off? How can you bless us this way when there are so many who have nothing? How, Lord? Is it even right?" I simply stood in the silence of the morning, my heart aching with His for the millions of poor, when the gentle assurance of the Holy Spirit chased away the guilt of having plenty.

"Andy, this house is a gift from Me to you and your family. This is not from YWAM, or the church, or your supporters or your clever ability. It's from Me. I have seen your labor for Me, and in relationship to where you live, right here in your own culture, I want to bless you. This house will be a testimony of My goodness to you for My name." Peace filled my heart. I could understand now with more clarity than ever the meaning of Hebrews 3:4, "For every house is built by someone, but the builder of all things is God."

As we worked, the money we needed to continue building came in when we needed it. Every month the church sent a newsletter out for us to inform and thank everyone for the progress we were achieving. People we barely knew, who had never given to us before or since, were sending gifts to us with amazing stories of how God had burdened them to send a donation. I was extremely humbled by their generosity because every time we ran out of money, God inspired our faithful friends to send us the amount we needed. We continued to behold the faithful provision of the Lord as we specifically needed it, and usually not before.

I glanced at my watch and saw that it was 2:30 p.m. The August sun beat down on my head. I took my cap off and wiped the sweat from my forehead with a grimy sleeve. Every inch of my body was filthy and sore. I was exhausted. I had been working hard for over two months now, 16 hours a day, six days a week, and I was beginning to wear thin. Although things were taking shape fast, there was still so much more work to be done. I was tempted to collapse under the tree and take a nap, but resisted the urge and just chugged down a big cup of water before going back to work. There was so much to do. In addition to working on the exterior siding, I was also getting the inside ready for the guys who would be coming to do the sheetrock. If I could just make it two weeks more, then the sheetrock would be up to form the inside walls. Being able to see the walls and visualize the finished house would give me that extra burst of adrenaline I needed to keep working to complete it. I set my cup down, stretched, and with hammer in hand climbed the scaffold to get as much done as possible before supper time when I could take a few minutes to relax.

> Being able to see the walls and visualize the finished house would give me that extra burst of adrenaline...

A week later I watched with satisfaction as the guys put up the last piece of sheetrock. They weren't quite finished with their job yet, but things were starting to look better. As I ran my fingers along the smooth, white wall, I was reminded of something I needed to do that night. I pulled the ink pen out of my front shirt pocket and on my hand jotted down a note to myself so I wouldn't forget: "Call Sis."

Dianne Gay was my younger sister. We had always been

close growing up and still enjoyed keeping in touch. She had mentioned to me some time earlier that she wanted to hang some wallpaper for us, which was her own area of expertise and the way she earned her living. With the wall up, but still no trim or door jams to get in the way, this would be the perfect time to wallpaper if she still wanted to. I called her that night to see. After catching up on family news I asked her, "Gay, we are just now getting the last of the sheetrocking done. If you still want to hang some wallpaper for us, you'll probably want to do it pretty soon."

"Well, send me the blueprints, Andy, with notes where the kids' rooms will be, and I'll see what I can do." I did so and a few weeks later she showed up with my other sister, Nancy, who came along to assist in the job. She came with her van filled with rolls upon rolls of wallpaper, telling me she planned to do the whole house. Gay and Nancy went to work fast and furiously, and in four days hung 277 rolls of wallpaper to decorate nearly every room of our home. It looked as if the Lord was determined to make our house as beautiful as possible!

It must have been providence that my friend told me of a sale he read about in the newspaper. A big lumberyard in town was going out of business. Everything in the store would be sold at reduced prices starting at 30% off, with continued reduction over the next few weeks up to 50% off. It "just so happened" that the sale coincided almost perfectly with my building schedule. And, most of the items they were eager to get rid of were exactly what I was looking for: door knobs, ceiling fans, light fixtures, wall outlets, light bulbs, paint, and lots of other picky little things that usually end up costing more than you'd expect. Poor Mr. Lumberyard Owner—what if he had known it was the Lord closing his store for us?! (Hey – you never know!)

The only things that weren't included in the sale were

the cabinets, which disappointed me a bit because our kitchen cabinets were a big headache. I knew I was skilled in that type of carpentry, but laboring for countless hours over the tedious work of cabinetmaking did not appeal to a man who had just spent each day of his entire summer from dawn to dark building a house. I was just plain burnt out, tired and simply wanted to finish up and move in. Finished cabinets cost a fortune, but in my exhaustion I was begging the Lord to please make a way for me not to have to build them myself. But it was looking as if–exhausted or not–building the cabinets for our kitchen would indeed be my destiny.

It was nearing the end of the three-week sale at the lumberyard, so I drove there with my dwindling list to check out what remained. The next day everything in the store would drop to 50% off, and that's when I hoped to make my really big haul. I walked in the door and then, looking around, stopped dead in my tracks. There, across the store in a corner, were all the cabinets they had pulled from the sale weeks earlier. I scooted myself over there to see if my eyes really were telling me the truth. And sure enough, they were. There all around me were the cabinets that would not only fit in our new kitchen, but look great too. And tomorrow their cost would be knocked to half-price! With a quick prayer for an angel of the Lord to encamp around them, I hurried home to get all the exact kitchen measurements and organize a big enough truck so we could be there bright and early the next day, buy the cabinets and get them back to the house.

I raced over the next morning to join the hoards, desperately hoping that the cabinets were still there. No one had bought them yet, so I lost no haste in measuring and purchasing them on the spot. I left that store with an incredible deal. That evening I stood in my new kitchen with cupboards on the floor all around me, and I lifted my heart to the Lord in thanksgiving. He had heard the groan of my heart and was mercifully giving me a break. This was the boost of faith I needed to go the last mile and finish the house.

Those last few weeks seemed to take forever. The carpet and linoleum took a couple of days to lay with the assistance of some friends who offered their skills to help me. I then spent the rest of the time finishing the tedious jobs like painting, installing light fixtures, hanging doors, staining and nailing trim, and an abundance of other time-consuming jobs. Susie and the kids all helped with the work at the house, as well as cleaning and packing the mobile home in preparation for the big move. It was now the end of October and after four months and three weeks of intense labor, we were all pretty tired. It would be so good to finally move in and relax.

I had decided we were going to take communion together as a family this first night in our new house and invite the Holy Spirit to live here with us.

November 4, 1988 — Moving day. The guys from the base showed up at the mobile home in the morning to help load the boxes Susie and the girls had been packing all week. We piled everything into the garage, and by nightfall we were bidding the small mobile home–our home of eight years–farewell forever.

I walked into the house and just looked around. There were a lot of little things that still needed to be completed, but it was finished enough for us to move in. This was an awesome day for us. I watched as all the members of our family either scurried around in excitement or dropped to the floor in exhaustion. I went in search of Susie, finding her leaning against the kitchen counter staring tiredly at the wall as two or three of the children vied for her nonexistent attention to ask their ever-so-important questions.

I shooed them away and pulled Susie into my arms for a weary hug.

"You know, this is a big night for us, hon. The promise... God has really done it. Can you believe it? We need to get all the kids together and thank the Lord and commit this house to Him, don't you think?" She numbly nodded. I kissed the top of her head and went out to buy a bottle of grape juice at the corner store. I had decided we were going to take communion together as a family this first night in our new house and invite the Holy Spirit to live there with us.

Susie got out the crackers and paper cups to pour the juice while I rounded up the kids. We all gathered around the table—one of the few pieces of furniture in the house—and passed out the "bread" and "wine." I took in the scene of my disheveled family gathered in the dining room of our fulfilled promise: Corrie, ten now, trying to untangle her hair from baby Nicky's sticky little fingers; Jessica (five) was poking Melissa (seven) to wake her up, much to Melissa's irritation; twelve-year-old Ben was sneaking a sip of the grape juice, only to be caught by Gracie, who was now thirteen and had just completed her first outreach to Mexico without Mom and Dad; and Joey, our two-year-old, was squirming in his chair, prematurely eating his cracker. Susie closed the refrigerator door after putting the juice away, handed Joey another cracker and gave me a look as if to say, "O.K., I'm ready when you are." Determined to keep it short in spite of my long-winded nature, I hushed everyone and began the communion service. That first night we marked as a time of dedication, reaffirming the commitment we made to God's call on our lives, our future, our family—we rededicated ourselves to God for His kingdom and purposes. Together we thanked the Lord for the terrific house He had given us to use, realizing His promise was true:

"...there is no one who has left house or brothers or sisters or mother or father or children or farms, for My sake and for the gospel's sake, but that he shall receive a hundred times as much now in the present age, houses and brothers and sisters and mothers and children and farms, along with persecutions; and in the age to come eternal life." Mark 10:24-30.

"...and you know in all your hearts and in all your souls that not one of all the good words which the Lord your God spoke concerning you has failed; all have been fulfilled for you, not one of them has failed." Joshua 23:14

Chapter Twelve

THE HARVEST — OUR PART — YOUR PART

"The harvest is plentiful, but the laborers are few; therefore
beseech the Lord of the harvest to send out laborers into
His harvest." Luke 10:2

Why, then, have I written this book? God has done
some incredible things in and through our lives; yet I know
that in terms of thrill, our story can be far surpassed by the
thousands of other missionaries God is using in powerful
ways around the globe today. It's not that Susie and I have
reached some spiritual plateau of faith and favor, unattainable
to the "ordinary" Christian. Rather, these stories are to give
a glimpse into the struggles, choices, and victories of *one*
family that has been challenged by God to do the possible
and trust only Him, especially in the area of God's provision
for the basics to live. We've attempted to walk in obedience
to His call and to help fulfill the Lord's command to "go
into all the world." We've had our mountaintops of glorious
victory, and we've also wandered in the valley, discouraged
and faithless. After 28 years of trusting God for our finances,
we have seen the Lord's faithfulness just as the Scripture
says in Hebrews 13:5-6:

> Make sure that your character is free from the love
> of money, being content with what you have; for
> He Himself has said, "I will never desert you, nor

will I ever forsake you," so that we confidently say, "The Lord is my helper, I will not be afraid. What shall man do to me?"

We have never gone without the things we need. He's provided beyond all we could ask or think.[1]

Whether you're a supported missionary, sponsored Christian worker, or hold a normal job, this Scripture still holds true. This very issue—our natural concern for our daily bread, shelter, clothes and all the other things our society requires—was addressed by Jesus when He encouraged and exhorted His disciples in Luke 12:29-34:

> "And do not seek what you shall eat, and what you shall drink, and do not keep worrying. For all these things the nations of the world eagerly seek; but your Father knows that you need these things. But seek for His kingdom, and these things shall be added to you. Do not be afraid, little flock, for your Father has chosen gladly to give you the kingdom. Sell your possessions and give to charity; make yourselves purses which do not wear out, an unfailing treasure in heaven, where no thief comes near, nor moth destroys. For where your treasure is, there will your heart be also."

Jesus' words are valid. The Father knows that we need "these things," and He will be faithful to supply our need in whatever way and whatever quantity He chooses as He considers our highest and best. God may use a miraculous provision, a concerned friend or family member, or a Church Body committed to support you as a missionary. The key is this: we must continually seek His kingdom, not our own personal kingdoms. We must treasure only those things which Jesus considers valuable.

---

1. Romans 8:32; Ephesians 3:20

The testimony of God's faithfulness to us serves as a witness to the truth. As we continue to walk this path, by no means having "arrived," there is one thing we can say with absolute assurance. "He is the rewarder of those who diligently seek Him."[2] He is faithful to His word and will be faithful to all those who put their trust in Him and obey His calling on their lives. Some will obey by going, others by giving. Both will be doing their part in co-working with God.[3]

My purpose for writing this book is twofold: Firstly, I want to encourage you to seek God with all your heart and, when your part in spreading the Gospel is made clear to you, do not hesitate to obey. Do not allow the false security of money to handicap you in your obedience. Be obedient. Step forward and make your best plans. God has promised to feed you even as He has fed the sparrows, clothe you even as He has clothed the lilies, and supply all your needs in Christ Jesus.[4] It may be through "manna" provision by supplying our needs daily as He did for the children of Israel.[5] We pray as Jesus taught His disciples, "give us this day our daily bread", whether we work a job or serve in a Christian organization. *The important thing is not to let money, things, possessions, education, friends or any other thing replace Jesus as the Lord of our lives.* Take the first baby steps of obedience. Don't let the false security of a "real job" hold you back from obeying the call of God on your life. Jesus said, "For whoever does the will of God, he is my brother, sister and mother".[6] Obeying Jesus' call on your life is as much a "real job" as any profession on the face of the earth.

Secondly, I want to issue a bold challenge to the Church, Christian business people and professional leaders, as well as to the pastors and Church leaders. It's time to raise the banner before our congregations—"GO INTO ALL THE WORLD."[7]

It is urgent for pastors to lead the church in an un-

2. Hebrews 11:6 3. I Corinthians 3:19 4. Matthew. 6:27; Philippians 4:19
5. Deuteronomy 8:1-3 6. Mark 3:35 7. Mark 16:15

precedented thrust to reach the unreached with the Gospel of Jesus Christ in our generation. God has given pastors the responsibility of leading their people and directing their resources to fulfill the Great Commission.

I'm waiting for the day that pastors, ministry leaders and Christian business people will see to it that the individuals from their congregations who are called of God into missions have the adequate support and training they need to obey God's call.

I've met and counseled many highly qualified young people struggling financially because their support team have forgotten them and have not fully supported "their missionary". Doing whatever needs to be done on a home-church level to really get behind and lovingly support their missionary is critical for winning the millions who have never heard the gospel for the first time. *Almost as bad as a Church that does not send out missionaries, is the Church that sends them out, but does not take good care of them.* Whether they are on a foreign mission field or on staff with a faith mission organization, they need your love, prayers and practical support. Remember, we are all called together to Go.

Supporting missionaries in prayer and finances should be the whole congregation's commitment. This includes those with an abundance of resources, and those with a meager supply.[8] Jesus said:

> "Give and it will be given to you; good measure, pressed down, shaken together, running over, they will pour into your lap. For whatever measure you dael out to others, it will be dealt to you in return." Luke 6:38

So, church-going family, GIVE! Wealthy business people, GIVE! Church Missions Committee, GIVE! Anyone who values Jesus' words, principles, and desire to see Him return

---

8. Mark 12:41-44

GIVE! GIVE! GIVE![9] Don't forget: Where you put your treasure is a perfect indication of where your heart is.[10]

My firm conviction is that the Church of God is called to pray fervently and give generously to God's global agenda, until Matthew 24:14 is fulfilled:

> "And this gospel of the kingdom shall be preached
> in the whole world for a witness to all the nations,
> and then the end shall come."

Until then, we must keep pryaing, giving and going to the lost as fast and as often as we possibly can.

HE IS FAITHFUL!

The End

Note: The *White Knuckle Faith* Study Guide is available for personal discipleship and Go-Team support development. Please refer to the contact information at the end of this book to order.

---

9. Matthew 24:14; II Peter 3:10-13; II Corinthians 8:13-15; Acts 20: 34-35
10. Matthew 6:21

Final Comment

This book shares some of our *White Knuckle Faith* adventure. If you don't have a personal faith in the Lord Jesus then alot of what you have just read may seem unbelievable. Or maybe you wish you too could live such a life of faith. Well you can! Here's how to begin that friendship with Jesus now:

1. Realize that God loves you and has created you for a very unique purpose.[1]

2. Because He loves you, admit to God that you have sinned and ask Him to forgive you.[2]

3. Believe that God's perfect son, Jesus has completely taken your sin to the cross, where He died in your place. By rising from the dead, He gave you eternal life.[3]

4. Begin your eternal life today by inviting Jesus to live in you and through you each day. Ask Him to guide everything you do and say.[4]

5. Read the Bible regularly, so that you can begin to think the way God thinks. If you don't understand what you're reading, ask the Holy Spirit to make it clear to you.[5]

6. Hang out with other believers that love Jesus. If you don't know who those people are, ask God to lead you in finding friends that are genuine believers.[6]

I especially want to encourage those of you who are wondering how to obey the call of God. Seek God through

---

1. Psalm 139:13-16 2. I John 1:9 3. John 3:16 4. II Corinthians 6:2
5. Romans 12:2; II Timothy 3:16-17 6. Hebrews 10:23-25

fasting and praying. Study the Scriptures. Talk to your pastor, make a decision and by faith step out in what He has challenged your heart to do. Don't let the fears of others, lack of money or an uncertain future discourage you. (Many will not celebrate your obedience because of their own fears, but you must obey God's call in His time).

Each man is given a measure of faith, whether single or married.[7] So don't hesitate to obey His leading. God knows your needs and is able to make every provision. Don't accept the lie; "I'll wait until I can be completely self-supporting before I serve God full- time," or "When my family is fully grown, then I'll obey." If God is moving in your heart to be in full-time service, obey His call—He knows the best for you. Don't miss the stirring of God on your life. Like the waters at the pool of Bethesda, get in now while God's moving.[8] (See Appendix II for more guidance.)

Above all, don't be discouraged! Remember that it is God who is your provider and source. If God could provide for multitudes of Israelites in the wilderness, He can surely provide for you and your family.[9] Trust Him and be obedient to His direction. Pray and start your *White Knuckle Faith* adventure now!

---

7. Romans 12:1-3 8. John 5:2-4 9. Deuteronomy 1:29-33

Appendix I

A few years after our home was built and we were settled in, the local newspaper wrote the following article in their Sunday edition. The following is reprinted with permission.

'Builder of All Things' Inspires Two-Story, Seven-Child Home
By Heide Stambuck
News Staff Writer for The Morning News

The Andrew Huddleston family at Elm Springs is much bigger than Mom, Dad and seven kids. It includes people from around the country who pitched in four years ago and helped the Huddlestons build a house.

Huddleston, who is a counselor at International Missions Network Center (formerly Youth With A Mission) at Elm Springs, and his family are listed in today's issue of *USA Weekend*, the weekly magazine included in the Sunday edition of *The Morning News*. The magazine publishes an annual Family Spirit issue around Thanksgiving and this year's theme is "Family Working Together."

When he saw information about the issue asking for submissions, Huddleston, who wants to write a book on his missionary experiences, took it on as a writing assignment. In his letter, he described the family as unusual "in an ordinary sort of way."

He said when the family decided to take on the project of building a house, it wasn't a "pull yourself up by the bootstraps" type of thing. It was a miracle brought about by a spirit of community as family.

The six-bedroom, two-story, two-and-a-half bath house with 4,000 square feet including the garage was built in four months and three weeks and is paid for because the labor and most of the materials were donated by people the Huddlestons have met and worked with over the years.

Huddleston said a particular Bible verse served as a theme for the experience and as encouragement. It was Hebrews 3:4:

"For every house is built by someone, but the builder of all things is God."

Before moving to the spacious house, the family lived for eight years in a mobile home with two bedrooms. Two of the children slept on couches in the living room.

The family will soon mark their 15th year in Northwest Arkansas and, while they aren't missionaries in the traditional sense of working always in the field, it was only a few years ago that they realized they would be able to put down roots here. Huddleston's work with the missionary center involves training others for foreign missionary work and traveling to mission sites to assess needs and devise plans for action. Initially, the center's focus was primarily working in Central America but has been expanded to Eastern Europe.

The Huddleston children–Grace, 16, Ben, 15, Corrie, 13, Melissa, 10, Jessica, 8, Joey, 5 and Nicky, 3—and their mother, Susie, all helped in one way or another with the new house. Twelve years old at the time, son Ben worked daily with Huddleston, hammering nails and providing all kinds of manual assistance. Mother and older girls help by sweeping and painting and the younger children performed such task as sorting nails and even giving some help on digging a septic system.

"I tried to dig something, I remember, because I couldn't

get the dirt on the shovel," Melissa said.

The children also helped with keeping the outside clean and the landscaping.

The Huddlestons had two children when they became Christians and then missionaries. Susie Huddleston said one of the biggest struggles for her in making the decision to join the missionary field was the possibility that it would mean she wouldn't be able to have a house. She took the plunge, though, and her dream also came true.

"My heart's desire was always to have a house," she said. "There is Scripture that says forsake these things and you will receive them a thousand fold."

Andy Huddleston's father was a contractor so he was familiar with the business but had never built a house before. The quickness with which it came together built by volunteers was amazing even to people in the construction business, he said.

Friends came in on vacation, Huddleston said, and helped with the house. A stone mason did the rock work on the house, and Huddleston's sister put up 277 rolls of wallpaper. The architectural plans were modified by a friend from blueprints given to Huddleston several years before at a mission conference in Kansas City.

Double doors to a study in the front of the house came from a salvage store owned by a friend of a friend and had to be picked up at a time that Huddleston was going to Fort Worth, Texas, for another reason. An electrical contractor from Kentucky whose family was friends with the Huddlestons arranged for his company to take on the house as a special project. He and his two sons and Huddleston and Ben wired the house in three days.

The Huddlestons found out later that someone even paid someone else to help them get over a critical point. A Siloam Springs contractor offered advice on the project and made informal inspections. The contractor offered Huddleston a job after the house was finished.

Huddleston took a 90-day leave of absence to work on the house.

"I burnt the candle at both ends because I had to have it done by the end of that time," he said. "I didn't want to build a house this nice and this big, but I couldn't help it. The walls showed up, the doors showed up. …The dormer window upstairs wasn't in the plans, but someone suggested it."

Susie Huddleston said raising seven children in a mobile home ensured that the kids learned to get along, cooperate, share space.

"You knew, once you start grumbling, you'll be depressed," she said. "(The new house) has been such a big adjustment, but we are so grateful. For the first couple years, Andy and I were waiting for the owners to come home."

She still hasn't put up many pictures in the house, probably because she was never used to having any space for them. In the mobile home, the walls were lined to the ceiling with shelves.

"When I had a new baby, I thought what can I get rid of (to make space)," she said.

The building experience has also been useful for Ben, evident when he spent a month last summer with a youth group building playground equipment. Other kids were surprised at his skills, which he had learned during construction of the house.

"We were helped through discounts, cash donations," Huddleston said. "It was a community approach to meet a need. People saw the need and gave what they could."

"A neighbor told me, 'It will take you 20 years to pay off your friends.' I said I would rather pay them than a bank. In a mission, you've already given your life away so it wasn't scary to us."

"The Bible says if you seek the kingdom and His righteousness, then these things will follow. The 'then' came for us."

Appendix II

Several years ago I received a YWAM leadership letter with loving correction and instruction on receiving God's direction for life from Jim Stier. I believe he gave us a simple but profound view of Biblical understanding on direction. Jim pioneered Youth With A Mission's work in Brazil, served as President of YWAM for three years and is currently continuing to direct the ministry he founded in Brazil. He also serves on YWAM's International Leadership Team. The following is reprinted with permission. New International Version Scriptures are used.

A Simple Explanation on Receiving God's Direction
written by Jim Stier, adapted by Andy Huddleston

I've been praying and thinking about how we can do a better job of reaching the world and how I can do a better job of serving you. One of the results is this letter with some thoughts on *guidance and our lifelong calling.* Twenty-five years ago I was a Bible college graduate with almost no understanding of God's voice. Then He told me to join Youth With A Mission.

I arrived in YWAM during August of 1972 in Sunland, California. My first impression was that God had put me amongst some pretty strange people. They were always saying that God had spoken to them.

The only people I had heard talking like that before were guys who wanted to break up with their girlfriends and found it convenient to blame God.

Within days, however, I was drawn to the earnest commitment to obey God in detail. The practical application of this commitment was revolutionary for me. It's also been a great adventure, and I've seen countless miracles associated with hearing the voice of God.

However, as I have more recently looked at the global situation in YWAM I have come to feel that there is something missing in the paradigm which most of us seem to have used for guidance. I don't want to overstate the problem, but it seems to me that there are too many who are confused about what to do. As a result there is a certain lack of punch, perseverance and strategic movement. Our efforts to reach the unreached has progressed slowly. Many end up back home, frustrated and not really knowing what went wrong. *Others spend years going from one short-term activity to another without any significant sense of progress toward the finish line.* We as leaders must help our people to cope with lack of direction and to eventually achieve the deep satisfaction of knowing that they have finished the race, that they have fought the good fight.[1]

As a mission, God had us start in the Christian lands, places where potential missionaries and finances were abundant. We established our foundations. Now it is time to move out and add great works among the unreached. How do we move ahead in our focus if almost everyone's guidance seems to be limited to countries and peoples which they are already familiar with?

I think that there is help for us in the life and example of Paul. He was the first missionary, after all, and his life is especially applicable to a YWAMer. Paul didn't just ask God what his next step or activity was to be. *He had a guidance*

---

1. II Timothy 4:7

system composed of three distinct levels.

The two more general and foundational levels supported and gave stability and direction to the more immediate seeking of God for his next step.

First of all, Paul *supported all that he did out of the Scriptures* and out of redemptive history. In Romans 15:8-12 he uses Old Testament passages to support this work with the Gentiles. In Galatians 3:6–8 he points to the history of Israel to prove that God had the non-Jewish peoples in mind even at the very inception of his covenant with Abraham. *Paul was firmly anchored in the Bible and in history.* He had the facts.

People don't get guidance in a vacuum. I recently heard of a DTS director who decided to record the intercession targets of his students. He made a map of the world and used color-coded tacks to track how many times they had prayed for each target. *He discovered that the students were consistently guided to pray for the situations they knew the most about.* In other words, if they had known more they would probably have prayed for more diverse targets and for more unreached peoples. I believe that their ministry calling would also be influenced.

Let's turn all YWAM bases into places where knowledge about the nations and peoples is not only available *but unavoidable.* Our bases should visually express our commitment to reach the peoples. Our people should have an understanding of the history, theory, and imperatives of missions. *We can't tell people what to do, but we should help guide them by doing the best we can to supply them with all available historical and ethnic information.*

Let's make sure that our students and workers *are saturated with Biblical knowledge about God's purposes in the nations.* I don't mean a little motivational talk once in a while, but thorough studies. Paul submitted his life first to Scriptural guidance. He would not have invested his life into something which was against Scripture. He would not have invested his life in something which was of little importance to God in the Bible.

Paul added to his biblical knowledge *a strong conviction about his vocation here on earth. This was his second level of guidance.* He expressed his ultimate purpose in Romans 15:16:

> "to be a minister of Christ Jesus to the Gentiles with the priestly duty of proclaiming the gospel of God, so that the Gentiles might become an offering acceptable to God, sanctified by the Holy Spirit."

This never changed in Paul's life. No matter what the suffering and no matter what doubts and confusion he encountered, he had pre-established the purpose of his life, and he wasn't going to turn aside from it. He submitted his strategies to this life calling:

> "I will not venture to speak of anything except what Christ has accomplished through me in leading the Gentiles to obey God by what I have said and done by the power of signs and miracles, through the power of the Spirit." Romans 15:18

He submitted his decisions as to location to this ultimate purpose:

> "So from Jerusalem all the way round to Illyricum, I have fully proclaimed the gospel of Christ. It has always been my ambition to preach the gospel where Christ was not known, so that I would not be building on someone else's foundation. Rather, as it is written: 'Those who were not told about him will see, and those who have not heard will understand.'" Romans 15:19b-21

His sense of mission was so well defined that he even knew when he had reached the finish line. At the end of his life he could say, "I have fought the good fight, I have finished the race, I have kept the faith".[2]

The third level of guidance for Paul was the one upon which we seem to have mostly focused in YWAM. *He sought God about his next step, his next activity.*

This was the area where Paul suffered the greatest confusion. Once his decision to visit some converts was frustrated by the devil.[3] On another occasion two well-meaning initiatives were blocked by the Spirit of God until clarity was finally reached.[4] There was conflicting guidance regarding his trip to Jerusalem. He thought that it had to be done whatever the price.[5] A group of disciples, moved by the Spirit, urged him not to go.[6] Associates, motivated by what the Spirit had said, tried to convince him in a most dramatic manner that he shouldn't make the trip. They finally shrugged their shoulders in a fatalistic appeal to the will of God.[7]

The point is that *Paul wasn't always sure of the next step.* He was a lot like us in that he struggled to know what was the right thing to do short-term.

In the midst of this confusion, Paul was also going through almost inconceivable hardships. In 2 Corinthians 11:23–29 he gives us a description of his suffering, which is stunning in its intensity and duration. I've noticed that confused guidance combined with trying times in the ministry is a deadly duo which often puts an end to a promising missionary calling. *How did Paul keep steadfastly on course during all of this?*

When I was a young boy my dad used to take me trout fishing on Crystal Lake, near where we lived in Northern California. We couldn't afford a motor for the boat so we had to row around the lake. I was still quite young but always wanted to try my hand at the oars. Finally, one day Dad

---

2. II Timothy 4:71 3. I Thessalonians 2:17-18 4. Acts 16:6-10 5. Acts 20:22-24
6. Acts 21:3-4 7. Acts 21:11-14

let me. The result was a surge of triumphant anticipation followed swiftly by angry frustration.

Clambering into the seat between the oars with my back toward the prow, I made sure that the oars were in their locks and began to row, pulling the boat through the water. I immediately discovered that I couldn't keep the boat going in a straight line. No matter how carefully I made each pull on the oars, within a few strokes we were off course. It was a lot harder than it looked! My dad waited until I was well aware that I needed help and then taught me how it was done. He told me to pick a point far off. On that first day it was a big old pine snag on the far side of the lake. If I concentrated on keeping that snag directly behind the boat I could make tiny corrections with each stroke of the oars. The boat kept on course and we arrived at our destination.

Our lives are a lot like that. It's not enough to carefully consider the next step. No matter how careful we are, we need a long-term perspective with which to judge and *correct* the accumulation of our immediate decisions.

Paul used the biblical revelation of God's will and his strong sense of a lifetime mission. He was confused at times and suffered a great deal, *but there was always enough perspective, determination and grace to keep him on course.* He finished the race. It seems to me that we need to help our people to develop a firmer sense of their life's mission. We also need such a definition for ourselves.

Most start out in missions with a surge of anticipation and triumph similar to what I felt that day on the lake. God has called us! He trusts us! We have something significant to do! Often too that triumph is soon followed by confusion, drifting, trying to find something we like to do and finally quitting, disillusioned and disappointed.

No matter what we do, many will fail to follow through on their calling. Even so, I think that we could do better if we would more deliberately follow Paul's paradigm of guidance. *Our immediate leading is tested by our life's calling.* Our life calling is tested by biblical revelation.

Short-term confusion is of relatively little importance, since the long-term perspective keeps us on course. This way of looking at guidance is applicable to the corporate as well as the individual. Our bases and ministries should also work on this basis.

If we will look at things this way I believe that we will not only do our job better, but we will help our people to live in greater peace and joy as we go about extending the Kingdom of God.

I want nothing more than what Paul lived his life for. I pray that we as a mission can produce more and everlasting fruit,

> "...so that the Gentiles might become an offering acceptable to God, sanctified by the Holy Spirit."
> Romans 15:16

Epilogue

The Adventure Continues...

My Mission Statement

To train, equip and encourage young men and women in Biblical principles of discipleship so that their lives are reflections of Christ for the furtherance of the Gospel.

Furthermore, to prepare each person to be fully supported in prayer, finances and pastoral care to go the nations.

"O God, Thou has taught me from my youth; And I still declare Thy wondrous deeds... until I declare Thy strength to this generation, Thy power to all who are to come." Psalm 71:17-18

We enjoyed the house from November 1988 to August 1994 when we moved to Stonewall, Colorado to help pioneer a YWAM work there. During the six years we lived in our house in Arkansas, each child enjoyed the house with lots of room to play, laugh and grow. Our prophet's quarter was a quiet place for traveling ministers and missionaries to drop in and stay a few nights or weeks.

The two acres had our children playing, flying kites, romping with our dogs and pasturing horses and calves. Our family's communion service together giving the house back the first night we moved in was honored as we accepted God's call to move in 1994.

I continued to work throughout YWAM internationally while helping to pioneer the work in southern Colorado. The children got a taste of the Rocky Mountains as they finished their schooling and launched out into their own mission of life, some joining YWAM themselves, and others taking on a career with passion.

Presently we are settled in Kona, Hawaii, serving at the University of the Nations, which is a training hub of YWAM's expanding work around the world. From this campus, I hope to see breakthroughs in the discovery and development of new models of missionary support and project funding for our non-western staff and students. I also hope to be able to further develop, launch and multiply support models for the 21st century missionary via the internet.

Contact Information

To schedule speaking engagements, conferences, workshops and support team training seminars, contact the author directly at:

Andy Huddleston
University of the Nations/YWAM
75-5851 Kuakini Hwy. #194
Kailua-Kona, HI 96740

Phone Numbers:
University of the Nations/YWAM
Office: 808-326-4492

E-Mail: andy@whiteknucklefaith.com

White Knuckle Faith Go-Teams
Join a Go-Team by sponsoring a missionary or special project. Visit the website below to check out the young missionaries and opportunities.

Quantity Book Orders
To purchase quantity orders of *White Knuckle Faith* and other related products, please visit:

Website: www.whiteknucklefaith.com

Also available; *White Knuckle Faith* Study Guide for personal discipleship and Go-Team support development.

Printed in the United States
131497LV00001B/20/A